THE MAKING OF AN ARAB NATIONALIST

Princeton Studies on the Near East

The Making of AN ARAB NATIONALIST

OTTOMANISM AND ARABISM IN THE LIFE AND THOUGHT OF SATI' AL-HUSRI

By William L. Cleveland

PRINCETON, NEW JERSEY
PRINCETON UNIVERSITY PRESS
1971

Library of Congress Card No.: 78-155961
ISBN: 0-691-03088-x

This book is composed in Linotype Baskerville

Printed in the United States of America
by Princeton University Press
Princeton, New Jersey

TO MY PARENTS

A Note on Transliteration

Arabic transliteration has been kept simple in the text and only ʻayn and medial and terminal hamza have received diacritical marks. In addition, commonly accepted English forms have been used for Arabic names and terms when such forms exist. In the bibliography, however, full transliteration of Arab authors and titles has been given.

Acknowledgments

I should like to express my appreciation to a number of people whose assistance has helped make this study possible. I am indebted to Professor R. Bayly Winder of New York University who first introduced me to the topic of the present work and to Professor Cyril Black of Princeton University who provided, as he has for so many, perceptive criticism and valuable support. Professors L. Carl Brown and Norman Itzkowitz of Princeton contributed helpful suggestions and frequent encouragement through all stages of the manuscript—to them I am particularly grateful. I should also like to acknowledge the assistance which I have received in the translation of Turkish materials from my friend, Dr. Osman Faruk Loğoğlu.

Finally, I owe a special debt of gratitude to two people. One of these is Mr. Khaldun al-Husri who gave generously of his valuable time in reading an early draft of the manuscript and who answered my many questions about his father with the understanding of a son and the insight of a scholar. The other is my wife, Gretchen, who gave so much to this work.

Introduction

This study seeks to explore an aspect of Arab nationalism which entailed the transition from Ottomanism to Arabism as exemplified in the life and thought of Sati' al-Husri (1880–1968) who has long been recognized in the Arab world as one of the most outspoken exponents of secular pan-Arab nationalism. As educator, ideologue, prolific author, lecturer, and confidant of King Faysal, he exerted considerable influence on educated Arab opinion in the decades following the end of the First World War. What attention he has received from scholars has quite naturally been restricted to his Arab nationalist thought.[1] Such a focus does not, however, portray the broader context required for a more complete understanding of his intellectual development and his relationship to Arab society.

Many of the leading political and intellectual figures in the Arab states formed after World War I had received their training in Istanbul and had served the Ottoman Empire before, and sometimes during, the First World War.

1 See, for example, Sylvia Haim, *Arab Nationalism*, Berkeley, 1964, pp. 43-54; her "Islam and the Theory of Arab Nationalism," in Walter Z. Laqueur (ed.), *The Middle East in Transition*, New York, 1958, pp. 280-307; Albert Hourani, *Arabic Thought in the Liberal Age, 1798-1939*, London, 1962, pp. 311-316. The most detailed expositions of al-Husri's Arab nationalist ideas are found in Muhammad 'Abd al-Rahman Burj, *Sati' al-Husri*, Cairo, 1969; and L. M. Kenny, "Sati' al-Husri's Views on Arab Nationalism," *The Middle East Journal*, XVII, no. 3 (1963), pp. 231-256.

The relationship of this Ottoman background to Arabism, both in terms of the loyalty conflicts it raised and its effects on the shape of Arab nationalism, deserves more attention than it has yet received.[2] In this context a study of Sati' al-Husri is particularly valid: he was deeply rooted in Ottoman society yet became one of the first Muslim Arabs to articulate a doctrine of Arab nationalism and Arab unity based on completely secular bonds of loyalty to and identification with the concept of an Arab nation.

Al-Husri was educated in one of the leading schools of the Ottoman Empire. He became an imperial civil servant and identified with the vague doctrine of Ottomanism. During his career as a school teacher and government official in the Balkans and later as a prominent educator in Istanbul, he had little contact with the various Arab societies which were active prior to the First World War. Even after the outbreak of war and the declaration of the Arab revolt, al-Husri remained at his post in Istanbul. When the war ended with the Ottoman defeat, however, he adopted the cause of Arab nationalism and became one of its foremost advocates. In the chapters which follow, his evolution from Ottomanism to Arabism and an analysis of his subsequent articulation of Arab nationalism will provide the central focus for discussion.

Part One treats al-Husri's life against the background of conflicting ideological alternatives to which he and his con-

[2] C. Ernest Dawn has examined certain aspects of this relationship in a meaningful way. See his articles cited in the bibliography. An important contribution by Majid Khadduri, *Political Trends in the Arab World*, Baltimore, 1970, appeared after this work was completed. In his treatment of al-Husri on pp. 199-205, Professor Khadduri has made some observations on the connection between al-Husri's Ottoman experience and the characteristics of his Arabism which are similar to the conclusions reached separately by the present author.

temporaries were exposed. The first chapter traces the most significant of the various solutions which were proposed at the time for the preservation and consolidation of the Ottoman Empire and analyzes al-Husri's response to them on the basis of his education and experiences. Although the author has benefited from generous assistance in the translation of Turkish materials, he has not attempted a complete treatment of the Ottoman phase of al-Husri's career. There is sufficient evidence, however, to ascertain his position in and identification with Ottoman society.

The second chapter is concerned with al-Husri's involvement in the vicissitudes of the Arab nationalist movement following the First World War and his career is traced until his retirement in 1957. A survey of the development of Arab educational policies is beyond the scope of this work and al-Husri's deep concern with this subject has been approached primarily as it relates to his general nationalist doctrines.

In some respects, the emotional relationship between al-Husri's apparent Ottoman loyalties during the war and his wholehearted espousal of Arab nationalism immedately afterwards is difficult to determine. Although he has written numerous books on his ideas of Arab nationalism, al-Husri the inner man remains elusive. His published diary for the year 1920, *Yawm Maysalun* (The Day of Maysalun),[3] is a valuable historical source for the period but reveals little about the internal adjustment he may have had to make after adopting the cause of Arab nationalism. The same is true of his published memoirs, *Mudhakkirati fi al-'Iraq, 1921–1941* (My Memoirs in Iraq, 1921–1941).[4] They are

[3] New ed. enlarged, Beirut, n.d. [1964]. This work has been translated by Sidney Glazer, *The Day of Maysalun*, Washington, D.C., 1966.

[4] Vol. I, *1921-1927*, Beirut, 1967; Vol. II, *1927-1941*, Beirut, 1968.

filled with factual details but avoid any introspective analysis. In this respect, then, only tentative hypotheses based on somewhat limited data can be offered.[5]

The second chapter also makes certain comparisons between al-Husri and his contemporaries in Syria and Iraq. A general analysis of the emergence of *élites* in developing societies is not intended, but it is hoped that by examining the intellectual and social points of contact and divergence between al-Husri and other Ottoman Arabs, some additional understanding may be obtained on the relationship between Ottomanism and Arabism and al-Husri's intellectual contribution to the latter.

Part Two of this study concentrates on al-Husri's doctrines of Arab nationalism. His intellectual models and his general definitions are discussed in the third chapter. The fourth chapter deals with his analysis of imperialism, regionalism, and Islam and his proposals for the inculcation of historical pride and communal solidarity among the Arabs. The direction taken by his Arab nationalist thought and the significance of his contribution in this field are best understood if they are viewed predominantly within the context of the conditions prevailing in the eastern Arab world between the fall of Faysal's kingdom in Syria in 1920 and the emergence of Gamal 'Abd al-Nasser in 1952.[6] While it is true that the majority of al-Husri's books have appeared since 1940, it should be noted that many of the essays which they contain were presented in lectures and articles begin-

[5] Particularly useful in this respect are al-Husri's responses to the author's questionnaire, hereafter cited as al-Husri, *Questionnaire*.

[6] It should be noted at this point that although al-Husri included the entire Arabic speaking world in his schemes for unity, his efforts were concentrated on the area with which he was most familiar: Egypt, the Arabian peninsula, Syria, Iraq, Lebanon, Jordan, and Palestine. The present study reflects this concentration.

ning in the early 1920s. The basic structure of his ideas on Arab nationalism and unity remained unaltered throughout the course of four decades and his more recent writings are refinements or repetitions of arguments presented earlier. Although he recognized and responded to changing conditions during these decades and commented at length on events since 1952, this study is primarily concerned with al-Husri's intellectual role in the development of an ideology, and not with the political manifestations of that ideology. Therefore, his treatment of recent political developments will be considered only as it illuminates his general doctrines of nationalism. His driving motive was always the propagation of the sentiments needed to achieve Arab unity, and until unity was realized he felt that his original arguments on the subject were valid.

Contents

PART ONE

The Life of Sati' al-Husri, 1880–1968

CHAPTER

I

The Ottoman

Background

During the thirty years from the Congress of Berlin in 1878 to the Young Turk revolution of 1908 various efforts were made to preserve the Ottoman Empire from further territorial dismemberment and to seek a means of internal consolidation and cohesion. The success of these attempts depended on military and administrative reform and on the ability of the multinational, multireligious, multilingual Empire to evolve a comprehensive basis of loyalty on which Balkan nationalists, Western-oriented intellectuals, and Muslim religious authorities could focus. The reign of Sultan Abdülhamid II (1876–1909) was filled with the efforts of these groups to achieve a reorganization of loyalties along the lines of the different solutions which they put forth.

In the past, the Ottoman Empire had organized its peoples according to their religion, not their language or nationality. The basic personal loyalties of an individual were to his religious community (*millet*) and he was identified by his *millet* affiliation. In this system, there existed for example, a Greek Orthodox *millet* and a Jewish *millet,* but there were no Turkish, Arab, or Roumanian *millets.*[1] In the nineteenth century, however, this system was disrupted as the Greeks, Serbs, and Bulgarians began to rediscover their cultural heritage and to form ethnically and linguistically homogeneous national communities through political revolt. As Bernard Lewis has written, "new ideas from the West were affecting the very basis of group cohesion, creating new patterns of identity and loyalty and providing both the objectives and the formulation of new aspirations."[2] The success of the revolts of the Ottoman subject peoples, often under Great Power patronage, was such that, by the conclusion of the Congress of Berlin, the once extensive territory under direct Ottoman control in southeastern Europe had been reduced to Thrace, Albania, and parts of Macedonia.

There was a growing awareness among the sultan and various elements of the intelligentsia that vigorous new measures were needed. Certainly, attempts had been made before the reign of Abdülhamid II to halt the decay of the Empire. Institutional reforms as well as Western political and social concepts had been, however superficially, introduced into the Ottoman Empire during the Tanzimat of the nineteenth century.[3] The decrees of 1839 and 1856 had

[1] Bernard Lewis, *The Emergence of Modern Turkey,* London, 1961, p. 329; Lewis V. Thomas and Richard N. Frye, *The United States and Turkey and Iran,* Cambridge, Mass., 1951, p. 46.

[2] Bernard Lewis, "The Impact of the French Revolution on Turkey," *Journal of World History,* I, no. 1 (1953), p. 106. Even the intensive attempts to reform the *millets* in the 1860s served to emphasize rather than to diminish the religious, and to some extent, the national differences among the inhabitants of the Ottoman Empire. See Roderic Davison, *Reform in the Ottoman Empire, 1856-1876,* Princeton, 1963, pp. 114-135.

[3] For discussions of the Tanzimat reforms, see Davison, *Reform;* Lewis, *Emergence;* Niyazi Berkes, *The Development of Secularism in Turkey,* Montreal, 1964.

promised legal and administrative reform and had attempted to legislate an equality of citizenship among all the peoples of the Empire, irrespective of religion.

The concept of an Ottoman citizenship, like many of the other reforms, had its origins in Western European institutions. Through studies abroad and at the civil and military schools of the Empire, Ottoman intellectuals and officials became familiar with Europe, learned foreign languages, particularly French, and with increasing frequency embarked upon self-imposed journeys of exile when their experimentation with Western ideas attracted too much attention from the sultan. The fact that 1876 had seen the promulgation of an Ottoman constitution, however premature and forced it may have been, indicates the direction toward which some were looking in their hopes for reform. The magic words of constitutionalism, liberty, and progress denoted concepts which, while imperfectly understood and applied, seemed desirable in themselves and capable of curing the ills of the Empire. That the application of the 1876 constitution had failed was attributed by its supporters not to the inherent difficulties of forcing constitutional government on the Ottoman Empire, but rather to the absolutism of the sultan, Abdülhamid II, who had suspended it.

Indeed, the reign of Abdülhamid has justly been termed one of despotism,[4] but at the same time it was a period of searching, by both sultan and dissidents, for a focus of loyalty which could unite as large a section of the variegated Ottoman population as possible and so preserve the Empire. There was, however, disagreement on what this focus of loyalty should be. Was it to be based on Islam, on Ottomanism, on local autonomous ties which would be em-

[4] It was also, in its early stages, one of productive although centralized reform. See Lewis, *Emergence*, pp. 174-175.

braced within a larger Ottoman institutional framework? The result of this disagreement was a proliferation of leagues and societies, themselves frequently torn by internal dissension, intent on finding regeneration and new groupings for the continued existence of the Empire. A brief survey of the most important of these societies and the various solutions they put forth will help illustrate the intellectual climate of the Hamidian regime.

The first of these groups to be considered, the Young Ottomans, was organized in 1865 in Istanbul and ended its activities with the suspension of the constitution and the exile or defection of its principal spokesmen.[5] Although few in number and of minor importance in their time, their writings were to sustain the next generation and inspire it with a desire for liberty and a feeling of patriotism. The Young Ottomans objected to the bureaucratic centralization of the Ottoman Empire as represented by the leaders of the reform movement, Ali and Fuad Pashas, a centralization which they believed to be the cause of the Empire's increasingly weak position in relation to the West. Their primary goal was to introduce freedom and liberty into the Empire, to change "absolute rule into constitutional rule."[6] The intellectual leader of the group, Namık Kemal (1840–1888), sought to formulate cohesive elements around which a liberal Ottoman state could form and in doing so he introduced important new concepts into the minds of educated Ottomans.[7] It is to him that the popularization of the word *vatan* in the sense of fatherland is credited.[8] To Kemal, the fatherland consisted of emotional ties as well as geographic

[5] For a detailed account of the Young Ottomans, see Şerif Mardin, *The Genesis of Young Ottoman Thought*, Princeton, 1962.

[6] *Ibid.*, p. 13.

[7] For Namık Kemal, see *ibid.*, esp. pp. 283-336.

[8] *Ibid.*, p. 326.

territory, and in his sincere and romantic patriotism he articulated the notion of an imperial Ottoman citizenship in which the ideal of the union of the various peoples of the Empire, regardless of their race or religion, predominated.[9] But as Bernard Lewis makes clear, Kemal's use of the terms fatherland and Ottoman was confused and the word Ottoman tended to refer exclusively to Muslims. In spite of his appeals to non-Muslim citizens, "the entity which he served is ultimately Islamic."[10] Thus, while he could write about applying selected Western concepts to the Empire and expand on the idea of the common citizenship of all the Ottomans, he could also advocate a pan-Islamic unity in which the Ottoman Empire would take the lead in defending Islam against the threat of Western encroachment.[11] Kemal, then, left no doubt that he was a Muslim and that the ultimate focus of loyalty for the rejuvenation of the Empire would have to be based on Islam.

When Abdülhamid II came to power, he suppressed Kemal's doctrine of liberalism and expanded his Islamic ideas in a way that the patriotic poet and author had probably never intended. By intensifying his claim to be the caliph of Islam and urging the reunification of all Muslims in a single state, the sultan hoped to gain worldwide Muslim support against Western imperialism and at the same time strengthen the loyalty of the Muslims within the Empire to his person and to his program of repression against liberals and nationalists.[12]

[9] *Ibid.*, pp. 330-331.

[10] Bernard Lewis, *The Middle East and the West*, Bloomington, 1965, p. 78.

[11] Lewis, *Emergence*, p. 335.

[12] *Ibid.*, p. 336; Hourani, *Arabic Thought*, p. 106. For accounts of the influence of the ubiquitous and controversial Jamal al-Din al-Afghani on the revival of pan-Islamic doctrines in both Istanbul and

Naturally, this policy, while it might appeal to the Islamic peoples within the Empire, could have little unifying effect on the Balkan and Arab Christians, the Istanbul Armenians, or the Salonika Jews. What was needed was a more inclusive focus of loyalty, something that would preserve the remnants of empire, not split them. With this aim in mind, a group of students from the Military Medical School in Istanbul founded, in 1889, a society the immediate goals of which were the overthrow of Abdülhamid and the restoration of the constitution of all the Ottomans.[13] The society, called "Progress and Union," soon attracted new adherents and became active enough to feel the necessity of continuing in exile in Paris. The early members were all well acquainted with the proscribed works of the Young Ottomans, and views reminiscent of Namık Kemal were set forth as the program of the society by one of its leaders, Ahmed Rıza:

> We demand reforms, not especially for this or that province, but for the entire Empire, not in favor of a single nationality, but in favor of all the Ottomans, be they Jews, Christians, or Muslims. We wish to advance in the path of civilization, but we declare resolutely, we do not wish to advance other than in fortifying the Ottoman element and in respecting its own conditions of existence.[14]

In this was expressed both a desire to preserve the Ottoman Empire and to ensure that it remained, indeed, Ottoman.

This focus of loyalty around the idea of Ottomanism was

Cairo, see Hourani's *Arabic Thought*, chap. v; and Nikki Keddie, *An Islamic Response to Imperialism*, Berkeley, 1968.

[13] This society is thoroughly discussed in Ernest E. Ramsaur, *The Young Turks*, Princeton, 1957.

[14] Quoted in *ibid.*, p. 25, from an article in *Meşveret*, the Parisian journal of Progress and Union.

seen again during the 1902 Congress of Ottoman Liberals which met in Paris under the leadership of Rıza and Prince Sabaheddin, who had recently joined the movement in exile. The only viewpoint held in common by the delegates of various ethnic and religious backgrounds was a general dissatisfaction with the rule of Abdülhamid, and the congress soon split apart on national issues.[15] The disenchantment of the Christian minorities with the Muslim state could not be shored up by Sabaheddin's call for a vague Ottoman loyalty inextricably bound to Islam, nor by Ahmed Rıza's demand for the replacement of Abdülhamid by another member of the same family who, although serving under the revived constitution, would be both sultan and caliph of Islam.[16] Thus, the movement splintered, the two main leaders, Sabaheddin and Rıza, were left opposing each other as exiles in Paris, and Abdülhamid continued to reign in an Empire that could not become totally Muslim, Ottoman, or nationalist.

Despite the problems of sluggish reform and increasing repressions, the Arab provinces east of Suez appeared to be secure.[17] Tied to the Empire by religion, these provinces were relatively untouched by the influence of nationalism. Nevertheless, here, too, there existed a search for identity, a desire to meet the challenge of Western superiority with the strongest possible platform. And, as was the case with

15 *Ibid.*, pp. 65-69. 16 *Ibid.*, p. 73.

17 These provinces included the vilayets of Aleppo, Damascus, Beirut, Baghdad, Mosul, Yemen, and the Hejaz, and the two sanjaks of Lebanon and Jerusalem. Egypt had established a relatively independent position of nominal allegiance to Istanbul in the first half of the nineteenth century under Muhammad 'Ali. The British occupation of the country in 1882 further cut Egypt off from the Porte, although Cairo's comparatively liberal press laws did make it a journalistic center for exiles from both Istanbul and the Arab provinces.

the Ottoman Turkish intellectuals, the Arab search was primarily directed toward the preservation of the Empire.

For the great majority of Arabs who were Muslims this meant that the bases of loyalty and identity were articulated in Islamic terms. Thus, Muhammad 'Abduh, the leader of the Islamic reform movement in Egypt, sought, not Arab nationalism, but the inner revival of Islam. He devoted his intellectual efforts to an examination of how the Islamic religion could be reconciled with the demands of the modern world.[18] Rashid Rida, a Syrian who immigrated to Egypt and became one of 'Abduh's disciples, although he emphasized the crucial role of the Arabs in Islam, was "not then opposed to the existence of the Empire, and indeed thought it necessary for the Arab and Muslim peoples, since it alone could provide the strength which they needed to protect them against foreign pressure."[19]

This is not to say that there were no local demands for reform and decentralization in the Arab provinces, especially in Greater Syria where a concentration of Christians had had intensive contact with the West for several decades. The organization of a small society by a group of young Christian Arabs in Beirut in 1875 and its activities in circulating anti-Turkish pamphlets has been interpreted by one author as the beginning of a political movement directed toward separation from the Empire.[20] However,

[18] There are numerous works on Muhammad 'Abduh and his disciple, Rida. Among them, C. C. Adams, *Islam and Modernism in Egypt*, London, 1933; Malcolm H. Kerr, *Islamic Reform*, Berkeley, 1966. See also Haim, *Arab Nationalism*, pp. 16-25; Hourani, *Arabic Thought*, pp. 130-160, 222-244.

[19] Hourani, *Arabic Thought*, p. 240. Cf. C. Ernest Dawn, "From Ottomanism to Arabism," *The Review of Politics*, XXIII, no. 3 (1961), p. 391; Haim, *Arab Nationalism*, pp. 23-24.

[20] George Antonius, *The Arab Awakening*, New York, 1965, pp. 79-89.

other historians of this period have presented convincing evidence to the contrary and have shown that the society's political activity met with almost no sympathetic response and that even the most radical appeals for reform did not go beyond demands for autonomy or independence within the Ottoman framework.[21] Even Christian Arabs like Adib Ishaq (1856–1885), Ibrahim al-Yaziji (1847–1906), Ahmad Faris al-Shidyaq (1801–1887), and Butrus al-Bustani (1819–1883) defended Eastern civilization in terms of Islamic greatness and concentrated their efforts on Ottoman reform rather than on Arab separatism.[22] The majority of Arabs, even with their sense of cultural identity, were not yet prepared to abandon the larger political identity of the Ottoman Empire or the religious identity of Islam as represented by the sultan-caliph of that Empire for political Arabism.

The impetus which finally drove the Arabs into open political revolt was given by a group which, in its origins, had no intention of splitting the Ottoman Empire into its various ethnic components. The Young Turks were, in their opposition to Abdülhamid, the heirs of the Young Ottomans of Namık Kemal's day and were in contact with their compatriots abroad led by Ahmed Rıza and Prince Sabaheddin.[23] Mainly composed of young officers embittered by the poor record and miserable conditions of the army, the

[21] Haim, *Arab Nationalism*, pp. 3-6; A. L. Tibawi, *A Modern History of Syria including Lebanon and Palestine*, London, 1969, pp. 160-167; Zeine N. Zeine, *The Emergence of Arab Nationalism with a Background Study of Arab-Turkish Relations in the Near East*, rev. ed., Beirut, 1966, pp. 59-69.

[22] For discussions of these Christian Arab reformers and authors, see Antonius, *Arab Awakening*, pp. 45-51; Dawn, "Ottomanism to Arabism," pp. 394-397; Hourani, *Arabic Thought*, pp. 97-102.

[23] The initial activities of the various groupings are treated in Ramsaur, *Young Turks*; the struggle for political power after 1908 is carefully documented in Feroz Ahmad, *The Young Turks*, Oxford, 1969.

Young Turks were not content simply to protest in journals and congresses abroad. With central headquarters in Salonika, the society spread in cell groups to all the garrison towns of Macedonia within a few months of its formation in 1906. There was less sterile ideological debate among this group than among the Paris exiles. When the two organizations agreed to coordinate their activities in 1907 under the name "Committee of Union and Progress" (CUP), their goal was plainly stated: "The fundamental purpose being to bring into force and continue the constitution of Mithat Pasha published in 1292 (1876)."[24] What sounded on the surface like an echo of Kemal's and Sabaheddin's Ottoman-based rejuvenation was to result in something quite different as the summer of 1908 began and warnings came out that the sultan was growing suspicious of activities among the officers of the Third Army based in Salonika.

It was against this background of absolutism, conspiracy, and conflicting concepts of reform, Westernization, Ottomanism, and Islamic revival that Sati' al-Husri was born and grew to manhood. His response to these trends, and his gradual and perhaps incomplete reconciliation of the conflicts embodied in his own person as an Istanbul-trained Muslim Arab will now be traced.

The Early Years, 1880–1908

Sati' al-Husri's father, Muhammad Hilal ibn al-Sayyid Mustafa al-Husri, was one of many Arabs whose lives were spent in the civil service of the Ottoman Empire. The son of a well-established commercial family in Aleppo, Muhammad Hilal was born in 1840 and received the best tradi-

[24] Cited in Ramsaur, *Young Turks*, p. 23.

tional education that was then available. He studied Arabic and the *Shari'ah* at the Isma'iliyyah School in Aleppo and then obtained a degree in Cairo from al-Azhar University, the citadel of Islamic learning. After completing his studies, he returned to Aleppo where he held the position of *qadi* in various towns of the vilayet. He married Fatimah bint 'Abd al-Rahman al-Hanīfī who was also from Aleppo and who was related on her mother's side to the noted al-Jabiri family of the city.[25]

At this time the Ottoman Empire was in the process of a piecemeal reorganization of its judicial system. One of the products of this reform was the establishment of a new system of penal laws and courts.[26] Muhammad Hilal, because of his experience and fine record in the *Shari'ah* courts of Aleppo, was encouraged to take the examinations necessary to qualify him for a position in the new courts. After a successful performance in the examinations, he was appointed Director of the Court of Criminal Appeals (*Mahkame-i İstinaf Reisi*) in Sana, the capital of the vilayet of Yemen

25 All information on the family is taken from pp. 1-2 of a 15-page mimeographed information paper given me by Sati' al-Husri entitled *Khulasah tarjamah hal Sati' al-Husri* (A Biographical Summary of Sati' al-Husri), hereafter referred to as al-Husri, *Khulasah*; and from p. 19 of al-Husri, *Questionnaire*. The al-Husri and al-Hanīfī family names do not appear in the last volume (covering the years A.H. 1173-1345 [A.D. 1759-1926]) of Muhammad Raghib al-Tabbakh, *A'lam al-nubula' bi ta'rikh Halab al-shahba'* (The Outstanding Nobles in the History of Aleppo), 7 vols., Aleppo, 1923-1926, although al-Jabiri is represented by several entries.

26 The new penal laws were a continuation of the work of the jurist, religious scholar, and civil functionary, Ahmed Cevdet Pasha. In a series of reforms, Cevdet Pasha arranged for the establishment of secular, or *Nizami* courts with their own judiciary and courts of appeal. Muhammad Hilal's post in Yemen was in one of these *Nizami* courts. On the courts and Cevdet Pasha, see Davison, *Reform*, p. 255; Lewis, *Emergence*, p. 120.

which had only recently come under tightened Ottoman control. It was there that his third son, Mustafa Sati' ibn Muhammad Hilal al-Husri was born in 1880.[27]

The first thirteen years of Sati''s life were spent in almost constant travel in various vilayets of the Ottoman Empire as his father was frequently transferred. After two years in Yemen, Muhammad Hilal took his family with him first to Adana, then to Ankara, to Tripoli in Libya, back to Yemen, and finally to Konya.[28]

Because of these numerous changes of residence, Sati' did not receive formal elementary school training in the *madrasah* with all the rote learning of the Quran and Islamic studies that such training implied at that time. In fact, he remained a basically secular man all his life. His education took place in the home where the language spoken was the Turkish of the educated Ottoman classes as well as Arabic—not until 1919 did Sati' make Arabic his first language. In addition, he learned French from his two older brothers, Bashir Majdi and Badi' Nuri.[29]

It was a remarkable family and served the Ottomans well. Bashir Majdi, the eldest son, held the position of public prosecutor in Homs and Benghazi during the 1890s. Little

[27] In an interview with the author on September 28, 1966, Sati' al-Husri confirmed the correct date and place of his birth. There has been some uncertainty about this on the part of scholars. Kenny in "al-Husri's Views," p. 231, states that al-Husri was born in Aleppo in 1879; Hilmi Ziya Ülken maintains that the date was 1884 in his *Türkiyede Çağdaş Düşünce Tarihi* (Contemporary Intellectual History in Turkey), I, Konya, 1966, p. 269. During his Ottoman career, Sati' al-Husri was not identified by his family name—he was known simply as Sati' or Mustafa Sati'.

[28] There is no evidence that Muhammad Hilal was politically dangerous as these shifting appointments far from the center of power might indicate.

[29] Al-Husri, *Khulasah*, p. 2.

is known about his education or his subsequent career. Badi' Nuri, who was four years older than Sati', attended the Mülkiye Mektebi in Istanbul and went on to become a Director in the municipal government of the Ottoman capital as well as a noted author of books and articles urging social and economic reform. Eventually he achieved the position of *mutasarrıf,* which was second only to the *vali,* or governor, of a province. In 1913, while *mutasarrıf* of Nasiriyyah in the Basra vilayet, he was accidentally killed in the political murder of the commander of the Basra garrison, Farid Bey, by al-Sayyid Talib al-Naqib's men.[30]

Sati', like the other members of his family, was directed toward a career in the Ottoman bureaucracy. The formal education intended to prepare him for this position began in 1893 when Muhammad Hilal, after once again being transferred to Western Tripoli, enrolled his youngest son in the Mülkiye Mektebi in Istanbul. Founded in 1859 and reorganized along modern lines in 1877, the Mülkiye was a civil and basically secular institution designed specifically to train persons for service in the Ottoman bureaucracy.[31]

[30] *Ibid.*, p. 2; al-Husri, *Questionnaire*, pp. 3, 19. There is a brief biographical summary of Badi' Nuri in Ali Çankaya, *Mülkiye Tarihi ve Mülkiyeliler* (A History of the Mülkiye and Its Graduates), II, Ankara, 1954, pp. 325-326. A statement attributed to Badi' Nuri on the urgent duty of the Ottoman government to embark on a program of reforms is reported in Tawfiq 'Ali Burru, *al-'Arab wa al-turk fi al-'ahd al-dusturi al-'uthmani, 1908-1914* (The Arabs and the Turks During the Ottoman Constitutional Period), Cairo, 1960, p. 440. The details of Badi''s death and the friction between the Unionist General Farid Bey and the independent-minded notable of Basra, al-Sayyid Talib, can be found in Sulayman al-Faydi, *Fi ghamrat al-nidal* (In the Midst of the Struggle), Baghdad, 1952, pp. 108-114.

[31] For an account of the role of the Mülkiye in the Ottoman educational system and a general breakdown on the recruitment and career patterns of its students from 1860 to 1909, see Andreas M. Kazamias, *Education and the Quest for Modernity in Turkey,* London, 1966, pp. 87-91.

Even during Abdülhamid II's rule the Mülkiye was a center of intellectual ferment, and several future Young Turk leaders were introduced to the concepts of freedom and patriotism through the initiative of certain teachers at the school.[32] How much of this Sati' absorbed and to what degree he was later influenced by the atmosphere of the Mülkiye are matters which cannot be traced directly.

Certainly, his seven years at the institution, three of secondary and four of higher training, do not reflect an attraction for active participation in politically oriented societies. Although he became acquainted with the secret publications of Ahmed Rıza and read the inspiring poetry of Tevfik Fikret while at the Mülkiye, Sati' at first used his knowledge of a foreign language to discover the secrets of Western science and mathematics rather than constitutionalism and patriotism. He so excelled in mathematics during his secondary years that he took extra courses in this subject at the War College and the Engineering School, earning for himself the nickname Archimedes from his colleagues.[33] His other courses ranged from botany to Ottoman history and also included intensive instruction in French.[34]

But this initial enthusiasm changed and Sati''s intellectual and career objectives began to diverge from those originally intended for him once he became acquainted with certain French works on the history of scientific discovery. He has noted how he was forced to continue with his required studies at the Mülkiye during the day but spent his evenings at home immersing himself in the natural sciences.[35] His

32 Lewis, *Emergence*, p. 192.

33 Al-Husri, *Khulasah*, p. 2; *Questionnaire*, p. 7.

34 A complete list of the courses, both secondary and higher, offered to Sati''s graduation class of 1900 may be found in Çankaya, *Mülkiye*, I, pp. 326-327.

35 His father had moved to Istanbul in 1896 when Badi' Nuri grad-

involvement in this subject became such that by the time he was graduated with distinction in 1900, he had no desire to work in the administrative positions for which his degree qualified him. Instead he felt that he should devote his life to spreading an understanding of the natural sciences in the manner of his model at that time, Louis Figuier.[36] A request to the Ministry of Education proved successful, and Sati' was appointed a teacher of natural science in a secondary school in the vilayet of Yanya, near the present Greek-Albanian border.

He remained in the Balkans for eight years, a period which exerted a profound influence on his thinking and reoriented his intellectual pursuits more toward the social sciences and the unlimited possibilities which their proper application could play in the preservation and reorganization of the Ottoman Empire. At the same time, he grew more politically conscious and his career became closely connected with the anti-Hamidian factions then present in Ottoman Europe. Significantly for the future, Sati' also became acutely aware of the motive force of nationalism.

For five years he taught in Yanya and at first the experience seemed a perfect fulfillment of his hopes. His contributions included the establishment of a natural science museum and the authorship of several books and articles on the subject to which he had become so deeply committed. The four books which he published while in Yanya were adopted for use by all the elementary and sec-

---

uated from the Mülkiye. Sati', who had been boarding with his brother at the school, then moved in with his family which was living in the Erenköy district of the city. Al-Husri, *Khulasah*, pp. 3-4.

36 Louis Figuier (1814-1894) was a scientific popularizer and one of the first to publish a scientific column in the French daily press.

ondary schools of the Empire.[37] In this regard, Sati' was principally concerned with what he felt were improper and outmoded methods of teaching the natural sciences and his publications attempted to make the subject both stimulating and scientifically accurate.

But as his concern for proper teaching methods increased, so did his criticism of the practices then in use in the Ottoman system. This brought Sati' to the attention of the censors and he began to experience a growing feeling of the impotence of his position, of the impossibility of proceeding with the reforms he thought were necessary while a teacher in an educational system that was growing daily more restrictive. Through correspondence with friends, he had learned of the exciting developments taking place in Macedonia since it had come under international supervision in 1903.[38]

Motivated by the prospect of being able to carry out productive reform, Sati' left the teaching profession in 1905 and took an appointment as *kaymakam** in the Macedonian vilayet of Kosova which was near the Bulgarian border and in the Austrian sphere of international supervision. Here the enthusiastic young *kaymakam* soon learned that not all

[37] Al-Husri, *Khulasah*, p. 3; Ülken, *Tarihi*, I, p. 271. The four books were: *Malumat-i Ziraiye* (Agricultural Practices); *Eşya Dersleri* (The Study of Things); *İlm-i Hayvan* (Zoology); and *İlm-i Nebat* (Botany).

[38] A decade of terrorist violence in Macedonia culminated in the I.M.R.O. revolt of 1903. Subsequently, Russia and Austria, with the sanction of the other Great Powers, drew up a reform program for Macedonia (the Mürzsteg Agreement) which included the installation of a European gendarmerie. An account of these events may be found in M. S. Anderson, *The Eastern Question, 1774-1923*, London, 1966, pp. 268-272.

* A *kaymakam* was the official in charge of the administrative division of a vilayet called a *kaza*. It was the second subdivision of the vilayet, and the *kaymakam* was subordinate to the *mutasarrıf* and the *vali*.

the necessary changes could be quickly undertaken. He later wrote of how he studied the conditions of his district and gathered conclusive evidence concerning the corrupt behavior of some of the officials there. In a report to the *vali,* Sati' urged the dismissal of these officials. When this correspondence proved ineffective, he journeyed to the capital of the vilayet in order to support his demands orally. He reported his mission as follows: "I was astounded when the *vali* met my explanations with these words: 'I know my son, I know that here, too, in the center of the vilayet there are found examples of the type of official which you have mentioned. I know that among the employees who surround me here there are weaklings and corrupt ones. But what can be done? I close my eyes at their actions and you, too, should close your eyes.' "[39]

A year later when Sati' was transferred to the *kaza* of Florina in the vilayet of Manastir he was made aware of other aspects of the Ottoman situation. Located in the sphere of Italian supervision, Florina was a center of activity for Greek and Bulgarian rebel bands. It was here that Sati' experienced his initial contact with a nationalism which he later described as "ferocious struggles centering around church and school and aiming at the conquest of church and school" through linguistic indoctrination.[40] He

[39] Al-Husri, *Safahat min al-madi al-qarib* (Pages from the Recent Past), Beirut, 1948, pp. 115-116. The *vali* of Kosova at this time was Mahmud Şevket Pasha who later played a leading role in the revolt of 1908 and the events which followed. He commanded the "Army of Deliverance" which marched from Salonika to Istanbul to put down a counterrevolution in favor of Abdülhamid in 1909 and later served as Grand Vezir for six months until his murder in June 1913. See Lewis, *Emergence*, pp. 212-215, 220-221.

[40] Al-Husri, *Muhadarat fi nushu' al-fikrah al-qawmiyyah* (Lectures on the Growth of the Nationalist Idea), Cairo, 1951, p. 97. See also, his

was profoundly impressed by the emphasis placed on the national language in education and by the attempts of the warring nationalities to gain adherents in this manner.

In addition to being the scene of competing nationalisms, Manastir was, by 1907, a center of Young Turk army officer activities second only to Salonika.[41] Although never a formal member of the Committee of Union and Progress, Sati' was nevertheless contacted by the society during his two years in Manastir. The methods of this contact and the officers with whom he was friendly are not known. He was highly sympathetic to the CUP, however, believing as it did that the substitution of the restored constitution for the rule of Abdülhamid was the best means for preserving the Ottoman Empire.[42] As plans for revolt became more definite, Sati''s involvement with CUP activities in Manastir appears to have deepened. When revolt broke out and the constitution was proclaimed in July 1908, the CUP called him to the town of Manastir, capital of the vilayet, and assigned him the task of receiving the delegations which came to announce their support of the Meşrutiyet (constitutional regime). Two of the speeches which he delivered on these occasions achieved wide circulation after their publication in the Manastir journal *Neyyir-i Hakikat* and

---

Hawl al-qawmiyyah al-'arabiyyah (On Arab Nationalism), Beirut, 1961, p. 101. Al-Husri further emphasized his reactions to this initial exposure to Balkan nationalism in an interview with the author on September 28, 1966.

41 Ramsaur, *Young Turks*, p. 114.

42 To what extent later writings reflect an attitude held at the time of events is difficult to determine. It should be noted, however, that al-Husri later referred with approval to attempts made before 1908 to end the reign of Abdülhamid II. See, for example, al-Husri, *Safahat min al-madi al-qarib*, pp. 78-89. See also al-Husri, *Khulasah*, p. 4, for his general disgust with Abdülhamid.

demonstrated the young man's hopes for a revitalized Empire of all the Ottomans.[43]

In welcoming the return of Niyazi, one of the leading army officers in the CUP, and his troops from the mountains where they had hidden arms, Sati' praised their activities, announced the constitution, and reminded all present that they should not forget Midhat Pasha and Namık Kemal whose work had made possible this glorious day.[44] On another occasion, he warmly greeted a delegation of Bulgarian bands which had come to pledge its support for the constitution, but managed to express, in the same speech, his sense of regret that some of them had agitated for Bulgarian independence or had sought inclusion in a foreign state without considering the interests of the Ottoman Empire. He then explained his belief that the initiation of reform programs under the constitution would reassure them of the Empire's good will.[45]

Because of a dislike for political maneuverings, Sati' soon resigned his position with the CUP in Manastir, declined the offer of an administrative appointment from Mahmud Şevket, and returned to Istanbul where he founded a short-lived journal, *Envar-i Ulum* (Lights of Science), and once again took up his educational activities which now promised to provide ample scope for his cherished reform policies. Nevertheless his relations with the CUP remained good, and Sati' emerged from the revolution of 1908 with substantial power and prestige which, coupled with his personal energy and his reformist outlook, soon made him one of the most influential educators and intellectuals in the Empire.

43 Al-Husri, *Khulasah*, p. 4; Ülken, *Tarihi*, I, p. 270.

44 Al-Husri, *Questionnaire*, pp. 5-6. On Niyazi, see Ahmad, *The Young Turks*, pp. 4-7; Ramsaur, *Young Turks*, pp. 134-135.

45 Al-Husri, *Questionnaire*, p. 6.

The Meşrutiyet, 1908–1918

The restoration of the constitution was received with approval in all parts of the Empire. Enver Bey, one of the Young Turk leaders and a future member of the ruling triumvirate, is reported to have exclaimed: "Henceforth . . . we are all brothers. There are no longer Bulgars, Greeks, Roumans, Jews, Mussulmans; under the same blue sky we are all equal, we glory in being Ottomans."[46] For a time it seemed that this dream would be realized; ethnic and religious distinctions were briefly forgotten as Bulgarian bands surrendered in support of the Meşrutiyet, Turk and Armenian embraced, and the Arabs of Istanbul and the provinces felt themselves to be integral participants in the new era.

But once in power and faced with the practical demands of governing, the Young Turks were unable to fulfill the hopes which had arisen. Politically, the Meşrutiyet was a time of conspiracies and power struggles, just as the preceding period had been. Abdülhamid was finally forced to abdicate in 1909 following an abortive counterrevolution, and was replaced as sultan by the Young Turk nominee, Mehmet V. Further power struggles ensued until 1913 when the CUP firmly established its leadership in the form of a virtual military dictatorship under the triumvirate of Enver, Cemal, and Talât.[47]

Moreover, external pressures against the Empire continued and denied the Young Turks the opportunity of internal consolidation. In the confusion created by the revolution, Bulgaria declared her independence in October

[46] Cited in Ramsaur, *Young Turks*, p. 137.

[47] A detailed treatment of the politics of the Meşrutiyet is presented in Ahmad, *The Young Turks*.

of 1908 and Austria-Hungary announced the annexation of Bosnia-Herzegovina shortly thereafter. From that time on, the months of peace were few: revolts in Yemen required expeditions in 1910 and 1911 which in turn alienated Arab opinion; these same years also witnessed serious uprisings in Muslim Albania; Tripoli was invaded by Italy in 1911; in 1912 and 1913 the Balkan Wars raged over Macedonia; and from 1914 to 1918 the Ottomans fought on the side of Germany in World War I.[48] Defeat in this latter conflict brought the final end of the Empire.

Hence, the downfall of Abdülhamid II and the election of a constituent assembly failed to guarantee automatically the success of the new era. Still, there were many who, in the face of the existing problems, continued to offer solutions for the maintenance of the Ottoman Empire. The Meşrutiyet was a stimulating period with the lifting of the Hamidian censorship. The debates of the intellectuals and officials were often ineffective, petty, and the result of incompletely digested Western concepts. Nevertheless, it was significant that they were now free to carry out these debates publicly. Journals, frequently of only a few issues' duration, multiplied and were filled with subjects never before discussed.[49] Responsible for founding at least two of these journals and a frequent contributor to many more, Sati' Bey rapidly achieved a prominent position among the

48 Accounts of these events, mainly from the point of view of European diplomacy, may be found in Anderson, *The Eastern Question*, chaps. X-XI; Ulrich Trumpener, *Germany and the Ottoman Empire, 1914-1918*, Princeton, 1968. A good survey of internal Balkan developments is that by L. S. Stavrianos, *The Balkans Since 1453*, New York, 1958.

49 For an analysis of the content of several of these journals, see Ahmed Emin [Yalman], *The Development of Modern Turkey as Measured by Its Press*, New York, 1914.

Istanbul political and intellectual community during the years of the Meşrutiyet.

Within this community, the current of debate was dominated by one crucial question: "How can this state be saved?"[50] It was a question to which answers had been offered before by the various groups and individuals discussed above, but the Meşrutiyet solutions differed in their intensified concern for the nature of the state which was to be saved.[51]

The terminology of classification becomes rather intricate during this period and can never be wholly accurate because of the way in which many individuals' beliefs tended to embrace more than one of the general ideologies. Ottomanism, which the Young Turks initially favored at the time of the revolt, indicated a desire to seek the Empire's regeneration within a unity which would include all Ottomans as equal citizens and in which the adoption of certain Western material achievements would insure survival and progress.[52] Although a Turkish nationalist could surely have favored selected Western concepts while an Islamist could have been inclined toward aspects of Ottomanism, historians have tended to use the term "Westernizer" to indicate one who favored Ottomanism and the application of European material and moral concepts while opposing the religious obscurantism associated with the Islamists. In this respect, Satiʻ's close friend, Tevfik Fikret (1867–1915) has been called the ideal type of Westernist, a utopian individualist who attacked the concept of the Islamic state and

50 Lewis, *Emergence*, p. 208.

51 *Ibid.*, p. 228.

52 It seems incorrect to term the revolt, as Ramsaur does, "a purely Turkish enterprise—a nationalist uprising," *Young Turks*, p. 147. For an Ottomanist interpretation of the early Young Turk policies, see Ahmad, *The Young Turks*, pp. 14-18; Berkes, *Development*, pp. 330-331.

argued for a new secular morality in which individual reason would overcome the stultifying effects of religion.[53] There was considerable exchange between Fikret and Sati', and the latter wrote that his first meeting with the famous poet and educator in 1908 quickly matured into a firm friendship in which their thought "grew closer together day after day."[54]

Opposed to the secular beliefs of Westernizers like Fikret and Sati' were the Islamists who argued that Islam was in no way responsible for the weakness of the Empire and that, in fact, Islam should maintain its primary role as the focus of loyalty for the Muslims within the Empire. Some Islamists recognized the necessity of borrowing technical knowledge from the West, but they continued to seek in pure Islam their political and social guide.[55]

A third and later focus of group identity, and one which differed markedly from anything which had been proposed before, called for an end to purely Ottoman and Islamic groupings and urged the recognition of the dominant position of Turks and Turkish culture within the Empire.[56] This was the notion of Turkism, or, in its most comprehensive manifestations, pan-Turkism which propounded the exist-

[53] From 1895 to 1901 Fikret edited the journal *Servet-i Fünün* (Treasure of Science) in which Western intellectual and social concepts were discussed. As director of the Galtasaray Lycée from 1908 to 1910 he forwarded an educational policy intended to produce patriotic youth imbued with civic and personal virtues. See "Tevfik Fikret" by Th. Menzel in *The Encyclopaedia of Islam*, 1st ed.; Berkes, *Development*, pp. 295, 300-302, 338-339, 406; Lewis, *Emergence*, pp. 188-189. Sati' included some of Fikret's patriotic poems in his Arabic writings. See, for example, *Safahat min al-madi al-qarib*, pp. 86-89; *al-Bilad al-'arabiyyah wa al-dawlah al-'uthmaniyyah* (The Arab Countries and the Ottoman Empire), 3rd ed., Beirut, 1965, p. 109. The friendship between the two men is described in al-Husri, *Questionnaire*, pp. 7-8.

[54] Al-Husri, *Questionnaire*, p. 7. [55] Lewis, *Emergence*, p. 230.

[56] *Ibid.*, pp. 228-229.

ence of a sovereign state embracing all the Turks of the world.[57] The intellectual foundations of this solution were established by Ziya Gökalp whose central argument was based on his observation that neither the Ottoman nor the Islamic approaches to the problems of the Empire were totally valid; what was needed, Gökalp maintained, was a regrouping around strictly Turkish cultural values and a reawakening of interest in linguistic and historical bonds.[58]

Given new impetus by the continued breakup of the Empire into its national components and the subsequent elimination of large portions of the non-Turkish element, by the actions of these non-Turkish nations during the Balkan Wars, and by the natural tendency of the CUP leadership toward governmental centralization in order to maintain that territory which remained, the policy of Turkism gradually became dominant after 1913.

The CUP's attempts to implement a policy of Turkification and tightened central control in place of the equality promised by the restoration of the constitution and the concept of Ottomanism clashed with the Arabs' sense of linguistic, religious, and cultural uniqueness and provided yet

[57] Pan-Turkism was a doctrine supported mainly by Russian Turks who sought to use it against Tsarist Russia. In the Istanbul community, Yusuf Akçura (1876-1935) was one of the more prominent of the Russian pan-Turkists. Sati' knew him and was familiar with his works on nationalism. Their acquaintance is related in al-Husri, *Questionnaire*, pp. 8-9. For Akçura's ideas, see Berkes, *Development*, pp. 321-322, 425-426; Lewis, *Emergence*, pp. 320-321; al-Husri, *al-Bilad al-'arabiyyah wa al-dawlah al-'uthmaniyyah*, pp. 121-123.

[58] On Gökalp and his theories, see Uriel Heyd, *Foundations of Turkish Nationalism*, London, 1950. Two important collections of his works are *The Principles of Turkism*, trans. and annotated by Robert Devereux, Leiden, 1968; and *Turkish Nationalism and Western Civilization*, trans. and ed. by Niyazi Berkes, London, 1959. Brief discussions of Turkism may also be found in Berkes, *Development*, pp. 343-346; and Lewis, *Emergence*, pp. 337-346.

another identification conflict for the Ottoman Arabs. Although a detailed discussion of the pre-war Arab movement is beyond the scope of the present study, its existence must be noted in order to give a complete picture of the range of intellectual and cultural alternatives with which Sati' was confronted.[59]

Arab agitation was prompted by a desire for reform and could not yet be called truly national. Upset by the imposed substitution of Turkish for Arabic in the local schools and administration, by the non-Arabic-speaking officials forced on them by the central government, by the dispatching of Arab troops to Yemen to fight other Arabs, and by what they felt were discriminatory election laws to the new parliament, Arab leaders began to assert their demands for reform and autonomy more strongly than before, both in parliament and through the formation of numerous clubs and societies. Principal among these societies were *al-Muntada al-adabi* (The Literary Club) of Istanbul, *Hizb al-lamarkaziyyah al-idariyyah al-'uthmani* (The Ottoman Party of Administrative Decentralization) of Cairo, and the two secret societies, *al-'Ahd* (The Covenant) composed of Arab military figures in Istanbul, and *al-Fatat* (The Youth) founded in Paris.[60] In addition, several reform societies were active in the leading cities of the Arab provinces.

While the programs of the various groups differed in the intensity with which they were presented, they were generally consistent in seeking reform within an Ottoman

[59] Comprehensive treatment of this movement is given by Antonius, *Arab Awakening*, pp. 101-125; Burru, *al-'Arab wa al-turk*; Haim, *Arab Nationalism*, pp. 31-34; Hourani, *Arabic Thought*, pp. 280-287; Zeine, *Emergence of Arab Nationalism*, pp. 83-115. For the attitude of the CUP, see Ahmad, *The Young Turks*, pp. 135-140.

[60] See Burru, *al-'Arab wa al-turk*, pp. 309-322; Antonius, *Arab Awakening*, pp. 108-112; Zeine, *Emergence of Arab Nationalism*, pp. 93-98.

framework. This can be seen in the resolutions passed by the Arab Paris Congress of 1913 during which statements of Arab desires for decentralization and equality were accompanied by declarations of loyalty to the Empire.[61] Still, the existence of strictly Arab societies and the continuance of their grievances, especially linguistic, created a sharpened sense of national awareness and a growing disenchantment with the Ottoman government.

Although he was a close friend of 'Abd al-Karim al-Khalil, the secretary of the Paris Congress and a leading figure in the Arab reform movement, Sati' refrained from involvement in Arab activities. He did give a speech to *al-Muntada al-adabi* at al-Khalil's request, but any commitment to a particularly Arab movement was lacking on his part. When al-Khalil suggested, with Talât Bey's approval, that Sati' serve as the Arab adviser to the Ottoman Ministry of Education in one of the new positions created to placate the Arabs after the Paris Congress, Sati' refused immediately.[62] He wanted no political association with either Arab separatists or Turkish nationalists. His response to the identification alternatives of the Meşrutiyet was that of a steadfast Westernizer and Ottomanist.

His most important contribution was in the field of education and he has been called the father of Turkish pedagogy because of his concern for the preparation of teachers equipped not only with knowledge of their subject, but also with an understanding of proper teaching methods.[63] However, his interests ranged beyond educational affairs and his ideas must be viewed within the scope

61 Tibawi, *Modern History of Syria*, pp. 203-206; Zeine, *Emergence of Arab Nationalism*, pp. 104-105.

62 Al-Husri, *Questionnaire*, pp. 12-13.

63 Berkes, *Development*, p. 405; Ülken, *Tarihi*, I, p. 270.

of the fundamental issues which circulated during the Meşrutiyet.

His first position after his return to Istanbul was that of Director of Darülmuallimin (Teachers' Training College), a post which he held from 1909 to 1912. With relentless thoroughness, he completely reorganized this institution, replacing all but three staff members with new, younger teachers who were more receptive to the modern teaching concepts which he wished to implement.[64] In addition, he introduced psychology and pedagogy into the curriculum, established a model school within the institution to test the effectiveness of his theories, and created a division to train teachers and directors for other teachers' schools in the vilayets. These policies established the young Director's reputation as a progressive and controversial innovator. Yusuf Akçura, the Russian pan-Turkist, commented in the journal *Türk Yurdu*: "When I visited Darülmuallimin the year following Sati' Bey's assumption of the Directorship, I found it basically transformed as if by a miracle. Although I differed with Sati' Bey in his views toward Ottomanism, I believed that the sound precepts with which he instilled his students would make them understand this error by their own accord. Therefore, whenever I met a Turkish youth coming from Russia or the Caucasus to study in Constantinople, I said to him: 'Try to enter the Darülmuallimin of Sati' Bey.' "[65]

The impact of Sati''s emphasis on improved, Western teaching methods was further increased by a journal, *Tedrisat-i İptidaiye Mecmuasi* (The Journal of Elementary Education), which he founded. This journal was completely

[64] For details on Sati''s reforms at Darülmuallimin, see al-Husri, *Khulasah*, pp. 6-7; Ülken, *Tarihi*, I, p. 270.

[65] Cited in al-Husri, *Questionnaire*, p. 9.

dominated by Sati' during the three years of his editorship (1909–1912). Divided into theoretical and practical sections, *Tedrisat-i İptidaiye* was a curious mixture of broad Western psychological and sociological concepts, detailed recommendations on the proper curricula, and examples of the most effective methods of classroom organization; it offered little compromise of its Western outlook to the Ottoman condition.[66]

In the course of his duties at Darülmuallimin, Sati' took two extensive trips to Europe in 1910 and 1911 in order to conduct research into European educational systems. He was impressed by the Europeans' propensity for hard work and by what he saw as an essential correlation between education and indigenous social and economic conditions. Yet he also observed that European material superiority was in no way based on innate mental advantages and he ridiculed the notion held by some educators that Ottoman children were incapable of learning by the same methods used in Europe.[67] It is not surprising that Sati' should have felt this way. Fluent in French and more familiar with European writers than with his own Islamic heritage, he was intellectually a European and was able to deal on equal terms with those whom he met, among whom was Charcot, the great French physician. He was never overawed by his experiences, and upon at least one occasion he was honored by his hosts when he was invited to become a charter member of the Rousseau Institute in Geneva.[68]

In 1912 Sati' resigned from the Directorship of Darülmuallimin over a dispute with the Minister of Educa-

66 The journal continued to be published by the directorship of Darülmuallimin until the 1920s.

67 Al-Husri, *Questionnaire*, pp. 15-16; interview with Khaldun al-Husri, September 12, 1967.

68 Al-Husri, *Khulasah*, p. 5.

tion.[69] He nevertheless continued to have a considerable innovating influence on Ottoman education. He held teaching positions in the Mülkiye Mektebi and Darülkhilafa, he founded a special nursery school along with an institution for the training of women teachers needed by the school, and he published another journal, *Terbiye* (Pedagogy), as well as several more books and articles.

With his concern for the individual, for the need to reexamine the moral and material bases of society through the educational system, Sati' represented a new type of reformer, the professional educator who sought to insure the future by properly motivating each student.[70] But the state which Sati' served in this role was not new and even his career pattern, although modified by the effects of the Young Turk revolt, fit into the mold of the Mülkiye tradition and he remained a part of the Ottoman system which his family had served. His writings, while they were professionally innovative, further demonstrated his commitment to the reform of the Ottoman state rather than to its transformation along national lines.

His initial public position after returning to Istanbul was that of an ideologically detached reformer and pedagogue. The works which he published between 1908 and 1912 reflected his concern with Western sociology, psychology, pedagogy, and ethnography and were generally lacking in any direct ideological content or political analysis. His principal models were Edmond Perrier, Albert Goudret, and

69 Al-Husri, *Questionnaire*, pp. 1-2. He regarded the policies of the Minister of Education, Emrullah Effendi, as disorganized, unplanned, and too uncritical in their application of the French system.

70 Cf. the discussion of this type of Westernizer in Berkes, *Development*, pp. 352, 405-406; and its explicit application to Sati' in Ilhan Başgöz and Howard E. Wilson, *Educational Problems in Turkey, 1920-1940*, Bloomington and The Hague, 1968, p. 27.

Charles Jean Marie Letourneau; he was also acquainted with the works of Demolins, Comte, Spencer, Renan, and Durkheim among others.[71] Sati''s individualism reflected the general Westernist outlook of the period as did his belief in scientific reason, progress, and a more secular role for religion in society.

One of his major concerns at this time was to show that Western moral concepts could be adopted within the Empire without resorting to Turkish nationalism. After his return from Europe in 1911, Sati' took part in a famous journalistic debate on the subject with Ziya Gökalp, a debate which has been called "one of the most exciting fights of the period."[72] Ostensibly about education, the societal implications of this debate went deeper and Sati''s Westernization and individualism were never far from the surface. In formulating his position, Gökalp contended that educators had previously been mistaken in taking psychology as their guide. They should instead, he felt, have given more consideration to sociology. This was because psychol-

71 Al-Husri, *Questionnaire*, p. 15; Ülken, *Tarihi*, I, pp. 270, 272. Perrier (1844-1921) was the author of several works on anatomical zoology and physiology, among them the 7-volume *Traité de zoologie*. Letourneau (1831-1902) wrote on sociological concepts while Goudret published articles on philosophy and ethnology in the journal *Revue Scientifique* which was available to Sati'. Demolins (1852-1907) was the author of *À quoi tient la supériorité des Anglo-Saxons?*, a work which first appeared in 1897 and in which the existence of individual initiative among Englishmen and Americans was posited as the reason for their success.

72 Berkes, *Development*, p. 409. Ülken remarks that debate was an essential element in Sati''s intellectual life and that he was one of the first Ottomans to debate in the style of Western writers. See his *Tarihi*, I, p. 271. For details of the Sati'-Gökalp debate, see Berkes, *Development*, pp. 409-410; Ülken, *Tarihi*, I, pp. 282-290. Gökalp's arguments can be found in Heyd, *Foundations*, pp. 48-70; Ziya Gökalp, *Turkish Nationalism*, pp. 235-247, 320, n. 14.

ogy viewed the individual as the object of education while sociology more correctly, in Gökalp's opinion, considered the nation as the educational object. For Gökalp, education should be national in the sense that it stressed not an individualistic approach to various personality and academic problems, but rather a collectivist inculcation of the particular Turkish national culture in which "the individual becomes a genuine personality only as he becomes a genuine representative of his culture."[73]

In reply to Gökalp, Sati' pointed out the uniqueness of the individual and the need to reform education around the true scientific spirit rather than simply making national culture into something which was a spiritual habit with the individual.[74] However, Sati''s opposition to Gökalp stemmed not only from this individualist philosophy, but more basically from his objection to the idea of Turkish nationalism which contradicted his own belief in Ottomanism, in the continued existence of a multinational empire in which the non-Turkish nationalities would still be able to make a contribution to the whole.[75]

As foreign pressure against the Empire increased, Sati' began to develop this belief more intensely and to offer solutions for the Empire's problems which were more comprehensive in their ideological content and more demanding in terms of his own self-identification.

[73] Gökalp, *Turkish Nationalism*, p. 243.

[74] Ülken, *Tarihi*, I, p. 284. Berkes has given this description of the debate: "At first it appeared that the two were sparring over pedagogical details, then a looping right of psychologism was countered by a short left of sociologism and they went into a clinch of Spencerian individualism versus Durkheim's collectivism." *Development*, p. 409.

[75] Similar ideas of Ottomanism and education were earlier expressed by Prince Sabaheddin who was strongly influenced by Demolins' glorification of the individual. See Ramsaur, *Young Turks*, pp. 82-87; Kazamias, *Education*, pp. 101-102.

Placing himself in the posture of agonizing self-appraisal characteristic of the true reformer, Sati' posed the question "Why are we backward?" pointing out the failure of the Ottomans to partake in the general progress of 'civilized nations.'[76] In elaborating on the reasons for this failure, however, Sati' was careful not to include anything basic to Ottoman civilization. Thus, although his personal allegiance to Islam was minimal in religious terms, he nevertheless clearly pointed out that the Islamic religion was in no way responsible for Ottoman backwardness; he explained that Islamic civilization was at one time a great world civilization and that religious reactionism and superstition rather than the essence of Islam had been the obstacles to Ottoman progress.[77] In an article of 1913 he wrote: "Reform is opposed not by that small minority which is knowledgeable about the essential rules of religion, but by that large majority who regard religion as a custom and view every innovation as evil and heresy."[78] In the same vein Sati', the Arab, rose to the defense of the Turks. He refuted those who said that the limited abilities of the Turkish race had caused the present retardation by pointing out that the Turks had known greatness in the past and were perfectly capable of demonstrating it again in the future. Nor had the Turks been negligent in their service to civilization for they, as well as the Arabs of course, had made notable contributions to the civilization of Islam through such scholars as Ibn Sina and Farabi and through the splendor of Bukhara.[79]

After eliminating these essential components of Ottoman

[76] Ülken, *Tarihi*, I, p. 276. [77] *Ibid.*, pp. 276-277.

[78] Cited in Yusuf Hikmet Bayur, *Türk Inkılâbı Tarihi*, II, part IV, Ankara, 1952, p. 468.

[79] Ülken, *Tarihi*, I, p. 277. Namık Kemal produced a similar argument in support of Ottomanism. See Lewis, *Emergence*, p. 330.

civilization as causes for the Empire's backwardness in relation to Europe, Sati' was able to point to what he believed to be the reasons for the present situation, namely a lack of the determination and persistence which were the primary signs of contemporary civilization. He argued that rather than slavishly copying the West, Ottoman reformers had been passive and uninformed in their attitude toward change: "We have waited for every step of reform until the knife reached the bone and as soon as the reasons that compelled us to take that step disappeared we have either retraced our steps or gone in another direction. . . . We have tried to remain stationary in the midst of the powerful floods that European life and civilization created in our country; we have not walked in these floods, but were dragged by them. Rather than looking like a person who is trying to walk or swim toward a particular goal in the flood of civilization, we have looked like an accident victim who wanted to remain motionless in this flood but was dragged involuntarily by the will of its currents."[80] What the Ottomans needed above all else, then, was persistent and systematic effort.[81]

In addition to calling for the rejuvenation of the Ottoman Empire through the adoption of Western values while retaining the essence of Ottoman civilization, Sati' also sought the Empire's salvation in an awakening of patriotism. His efforts to discover a motivating symbol with which to invigorate Ottoman education and society had led him to the

[80] Sati' was here refuting an article in which the journalist Yunus Nadi had deplored the Ottomans' enthusiastic imitation of the West. Sati''s arguments appeared in the journal *Içtihad,* May 15 and 22, 1913, and are cited in Bayur, *Türk Inkılâbı,* II, part IV, p. 467.

[81] The example given by Sati' in this instance was the labor, frustration, and eventual triumph of Newton in formulating the law of gravity. Ülken, *Tarihi,* I, p. 277.

belief that emotional identification with the territorial entity provided the dominating impetus for European progress and solidarity. He therefore sought to transfer a similar awareness to the Ottoman Empire. The five lectures which he delivered at Darülfünun (Istanbul University) during the Balkan Wars and which were published in 1913 under the title *Vatan İçin* (For the Fatherland) were significant in showing the depth of his understanding of European nationalism, his selectivity in applying its concepts to the Ottoman Empire, and the crystallization of his own loyalties around Ottomanism.

The lectures were, in general, a call for determination in time of defeat. He began by saying: "There are no better days than days of catastrophe to make people love the fatherland because such catastrophes have an awakening power."[82] He went on to explain that the patriotism demanded at such times possessed both a character and a feeling. It was to want the fatherland to progress materially and spiritually. It was a feeling of nostalgia when one was absent. But its essence was love of the fatherland.[83] To Sati', then, the term included much more than just the locale in which a person lived or was born. He spoke of a broad Ottoman fatherland and saw in patriotism (*vatanserverlik*) the spiritual sentiment equated with loyalty to this extended fatherland.[84]

Sati' followed this with a discussion on the historical development of the distinction between nation (*millet*) and

[82] *Ibid.*, p. 273. [83] *Ibid.*, pp. 273-274.

[84] Lewis notes that before Western concepts began to penetrate the Ottoman Empire in the nineteenth century, the political significance of *vatan* was no greater than that of the English word "home." See "French Revolution," pp. 107-108.

state (*devlet*).[85] He pointed out that fatherland and state were once identical, the king being the central focus of loyalty embracing both. He then explained how this concept changed once the notion of sovereignty resting in the nation came to dominate. His two principal models were France and Germany. In the former, he noted that fatherland was regarded as a product of history and will. Thus, for example, the people of Alsace, even though they spoke a dialect of German, had been historically a part of France and should be so again since they had expressed such a desire after the German occupation.[86] In Germany, on the other hand, where there was no tradition of a great state, it was necessary to resort to the tie of language in order to create a nation. The Germans regarded as German all those who spoke the German language, and the fatherland as the place where those people dwelt.

Sati' was also impressed by Japan's rapid awakening as symbolized by that country's military defeat of Russia in 1905. During his first visit to Europe in 1910, he obtained an audience at the Japanese embassy in Berlin to discuss this matter.[87] In *Vatan İçin* he drew the connection between emotional loyalty and national success when he stated that the victory over Russia indicated that there was a strong feeling of patriotism in Japan. Sati' felt that Japanese

[85] This discussion is found in Ülken, *Tarihi,* I, pp. 273-274. Sati' thus carefully demarcated the concepts of fatherland, nation—which had come to mean more than a religious community—and state. He refined these distinctions more sharply in his Arabic writings. See below, chap. III.

[86] This argument of "will" was taken from Ernest Renan. See below, pp. 106-108, for Sati''s rejection of the relevance of this theory for the Arabs.

[87] Al-Husri, *Questionnaire,* p. 16.

patriotism was inspired by a respect for ancestors and a belief in a familial relationship between the ancestors and the living members of the state.[88]

When Sati' turned his attention to an examination of the elements of patriotism needed by the Ottoman Empire in this time of crisis, he unhesitatingly identified himself with Ottomanism. His patriotic exhortations were intended for all Ottomans, not any particular ethnic or religious group, and his fatherland included all the Ottoman territories. Thus he selected only those elements of patriotism which were applicable to the entire Ottoman situation. He wrote, for example: "We cannot accept the concept of the Germans because language is the least of the ties which bind the Ottomans to one another."[89] Furthermore, argued Sati', Ottomans already have an independent state with pre-existing spiritual ties which override language differences. Despite his secularism, he was forced to define Islam as one of these principal ties since it continued to unite the majority of Ottomans. Still, he managed also to include the general patriotic emotions which he was beginning to perceive as the basic spiritual cement in modern nation states. In closing, Sati' referred to Fichte, the author who was the principal intellectual model for his future writings on Arab nationalism. Sati''s own self-view at this time cannot be ascertained with absolute certainty, but it is not without significance that the context in which he mentioned Fichte was the role played by his *Addresses to the German Nation* in awakening and sustaining German nationalism following the defeat at Jena.

88 Ülken, *Tarihi*, I, p. 274. Sati' subsequently wrote a book on Japan, *Japonya ve Japonyalılar*, and delivered a lecture which was published in book form together with a lecture on Germany by Faik Saleri as *Büyük Milletlerden Japonlar, Almanlar.*

89 *Ibid.*, p. 275.

It is necessary to remember that Sati' was aware of these concepts of nationalism at this time and that he could successfully manipulate them in such a way that he rejected Turkish and Arab nationalism and supported Ottomanism. During a period in which Arab discontent was increasing, Sati' remained very much a nonactivist in the movement, never joining any of the secret societies or clubs. His focus of loyalty was the comprehensive bond of Ottomanism and he desired the continued existence and rejuvenation of the Empire. In response to this author's inquiries, Sati' stated that he adhered to Ottomanism because he felt very strongly that the reform and progress of the Ottoman Empire meant the reform and progress of all its various components. Ottomanism itself was equated with inherent progress to Sati', and he wrote at the time: "The Ottomanism of the future will be provided in the schools of today."[90]

From a cultural and occupational as well as an intellectual position, Sati' had an interest in the maintenance of the Empire. An examination of the criteria which determined membership in the true Ottoman elite will indicate that Sati' Bey's credentials were perfectly suited to its requirements.[91] In order to be recognized as a true Ottoman, one had to use Ottoman Turkish speech, to follow the religion of Islam, to serve the Ottoman state, and to know the Ottoman way—that is, to practice the style of life demanded by the above. All of these outward manifestations were met by

[90] Al-Husri, *Questionnaire*, p. 4. As he was to do later in the Arab countries, Sati' recognized the importance of instilling patriotism in children through the educational system. He denied the validity of the Tuba tree approach which placed the reform of higher education before that of the elementary levels. For details on his views of Ottoman education, see Ülken, *Tarihi*, I, pp. 275-276, 280-290.

[91] This discussion is based on the framework provided by Lewis V. Thomas in Thomas and Fry, *The United States and Turkey*, pp. 46-47.

Sati': he as well as his immediate family had devoted their careers to the service of the Ottoman Empire; he was a Muslim; his first language was Ottoman Turkish; and he was educated in one of the most famous institutions of the Empire, an institution designed to perpetuate the Ottoman way. As a cosmopolitan Ottoman cut off from his Arabic origins linguistically and culturally, and in possession of substantial prestige and position, Sati' had a vested interest in the continued existence of the nonnational status quo.

The same was true of other Arab leaders of the post-World War I era who had had similar state educations and who held Ottoman government posts in 1914. Active support of Arabism was, in fact, given only by a minority of Arabs during the war.[92] In view of this, it is not surprising that Sati' rejected identification with Arab dissidents and remained in Istanbul. His position as a loyal Arab within the Empire was unique mainly in terms of the rank and importance of that position, comparable on a civilian level

[92] C. Ernest Dawn has systematically traced the loyalties of pre- and post-war Arab nationalists in Syria and found that an effective commitment to Arab nationalist activities was not a predominant factor until after the defeat of the Ottoman Empire. Even some of the pre-war nationalists served the Empire during the war. See his "The Rise of Arabism in Syria," *The Middle East Journal*, XVI, no. 2 (1962), pp. 145-168. Dawn has also shown that even Husayn ibn 'Ali under whose leadership the Arab revolt was proclaimed in 1916 favored association within the Ottoman Empire. According to Dawn's careful documentation, Husayn regarded Arabism as a political alternative to Ottomanism only because it promised to serve the same purposes for him which Ottomanism had. See C. Ernest Dawn, "The Amir of Mecca. Al-Husayn ibn 'Ali and the Origin of the Arab Revolt," *Proceedings of the American Philosophical Society*, CIV, no. 1 (1960), pp. 11-34. See also Majid Khadduri, "Aziz 'Ali Misri and the Arab Nationalist Movement," *St. Antony's Papers*, no. 17, *Middle Eastern Affairs*, no. 4, London, 1965, pp. 140-163, for a re-evaluation of the career of one who has been regarded as an initiator of the Arab nationalist movement before World War I.

perhaps only to that of Yasin al-Hashimi on the military level. And al-Hashimi, too, remained loyal to the Empire until after the Arab capture of Damascus in 1918.[93]

But the war was to put an end to the Ottoman Empire and to force those Arabs who had served it to re-examine their political and ideological loyalties. In the Arab provinces, Allied promises for the creation of an independent Arab state prompted the Sharif of Mecca, Husayn ibn 'Ali, to proclaim an Arab revolt against the Ottoman government. Allied and Arab armies led respectively by the British General, Allenby, and Husayn's son, Faysal, succeeded in capturing Damascus on October 1, 1918. The conflict between the Allies' desire to secure their own strategic interests in the Middle East and their willingness to implement their promises as interpreted by the Arabs was immediately apparent. While Faysal, assisted in part by several former Ottoman Arab army officers, struggled to set up a government in Damascus, the French and British remained in occupation of the Arab territories.[94]

In Istanbul and Anatolia as well, the Allies were in control. Following the Ottoman-Allied armistice of Mudros which was signed on October 30, 1918, the Allies estab-

[93] Yasin al-Hashimi (1884-1937) was an Iraqi who graduated from the Imperial War College in Istanbul and rose very rapidly in the military service. During World War I he served as Commander of the 20th Division in Galicia and as Commander of the Eighth Army in Palestine. When the Arabs entered Damascus, al Hashimi was captured and took that opportunity to become part of the Arab movement. He became one of the most powerful politicians in Iraq until his death. The most detailed work on al-Hashimi is Phebe Ann Marr, *Yasin al-Hashimi* (unpublished doctoral dissertation, Harvard University, 1967). See also, Khayri al-'Umari, *Shakhsiyat 'iraqiyyah* (Iraqi Personalities), I, Baghdad, 1955, pp. 101-135; 'Abd al-Fattah al-Yafi, *al-'Iraq bayn inqilabayn* (Iraq between Two Revolts), Beirut, 1938, pp. 82-86.

[94] Events in Faysal's Syria will be treated in more detail below, pp. 47-55.

lished a military administration in Istanbul. The British then occupied the Dardanelles, French and Italian forces took possession of territory in Cilicia and Antalya, and in May 1919 Greek troops landed at Smyrna. The Ottoman Empire was completely defeated and it seemed as if even its Turkish heartland would be partitioned. But the invasion by the Greeks, a former subject people, sparked a spirit of resistance among the Anatolian population. Led by Mustapha Kemal (Atatürk), a military struggle against the Greeks and a diplomatic offensive against the divided Allies ultimately proved successful and resulted in the establishment of the Republic of Turkey in 1923.[95]

The direct effect of these events on Sati', the Ottoman Arab, is difficult to determine. During the course of the war he continued his educational work in Istanbul, engaging in another long debate on the subject with Gökalp in 1918. How closely he followed the fortunes of the Arabs is a matter on which he has made little comment. He was naturally disturbed by Cemal Pasha's extreme security measures in Syria in the course of which some of his Arab friends, among them 'Abd al-Karim al-Khalil, were hanged.[96] Sati''s immediate reaction to the entrance of Faysal's army into Damascus or to the signing of the armistice of Mudros is not known.

[95] For events within the Ottoman Empire during the war, see Ahmed Emin [Yalman], *Turkey in the World War*, New Haven, 1930. Immediate post-war history is examined by Lewis, *Emergence*, pp. 234-250; Lord Kinross, *Atatürk*, New York, 1965, chaps. XV-XVIII; and the diplomacy of the period is examined in Anderson, *The Eastern Question*, pp. 361-387; Elie Kedourie, *England and the Middle East*, London, 1956.

[96] In Sati''s opinion, the death of this Arab leader, who favored Arab existence within an Ottoman framework, combined with Cemal's general policy of repression to alienate a large section of otherwise loyal Arabs. See al-Husri, *Nushu' al-fikrah al-qawmiyyah*, pp. 213-217.

It is reasonable to assume, however, that the months which followed constituted a difficult period for him. He was contacted by various Arab acquaintances and invited to join their ranks while at the same time he was urged by his Turkish friends to remain in Istanbul.[97] Muhammad Kurd 'Ali, who was in charge of organizing an educational council in Damascus for the Arabs, claims that he wrote to Sati' and urged him to come to Damascus to assume the directorship of Dar al-Mu'allimin. According to Kurd 'Ali, although Sati' did not answer the letter, his former students initiated an intensive propaganda campaign in his favor. As a result of this pressure, the Arab Military Governor of Damascus, Rida al-Rikabi, was forced to agree to Sati''s appointment as Director General of Education in Syria, a much more influential position than that which Kurd 'Ali had asked him to accept.[98] Sati' has disavowed any role in the initiation of the pressure on his behalf or subsequent political involvement with the parties which were responsible for it.[99] Aside from Kurd 'Ali's statement, there is no evidence that Sati' was actually invited to Damascus and promised the position of Director General of Education while he was still in Istanbul. Nevertheless, he certainly must have known that he was highly regarded by influential factions in Syria, and this knowledge could have played a significant part in his final decision.

[97] Al-Husri, *Questionnaire*, p. 20; al-Husri, *Khulasah*, p. 6.

[98] It is possible that Kurd 'Ali coveted the appointment of Director General for himself. He uses this story to illustrate how he was ignored by al-Rikabi after the military governor had persuaded him to take a position in Damascus in the first place. This episode is found in Muhammad Kurd 'Ali, *al-Mudhakkirat* (Memoirs), II, Damascus, 1948, pp. 277-278. Kurd 'Ali did become Director of the Arab Academy in Damascus and served with distinction in that capacity from 1920 until his death in 1953.

[99] Al-Husri, *Questionnaire*, p. 20.

Yet Sati' Bey's life and career were centered in Istanbul, and his most intimate friends were there. Articles appeared in the newspapers asking him to remain.[100] His already deep personal and cultural ties to the city were increased by his marriage, early in 1919, to Jamilah, the daughter of Hüseyin Hüsnü Pasha, a high ranking figure in the Ottoman admiralty.[101] Jamilah was a lively and well-educated woman, conversant in English and French as well as Ottoman Turkish. According to their son, Khaldun, his mother had strong attachments to Turkey and would most likely have preferred to remain there.[102] It is not known, however, to what extent family ties made themselves felt at this time. Sati''s parents were no longer living and very little information has been obtained on his wife's family. Possessions do not seem to have been a factor holding him in Istanbul. He had no personal wealth and he had usually lived in the facilities provided by the various academic institutions with which he was associated.

Whether or not he could have lived a meaningful life in the new Turkey is beside the point. The creation of a Turk-

100 Al-Husri, *Khulasah*, p. 6. When he finally left for Damascus, the Istanbul paper *Vakt* reported, "Syria has been severed from us." Al-Husri, *Questionnaire*, p. 20.

101 Hüsnü Pasha (1852-1918) became a naval officer in 1871 and held a variety of Mediterranean commands until 1898 when he became head of the Ottoman Naval College. After the announcement of the Meşrutiyet, he served briefly as Minister of the Navy in the cabinet of Kamil Pasha. Noted for his honesty during a period of corruption, he did not enrich himself from his high positions and spent his last years in hardship. *Türk Meşhurları* (Famous Turks). Istanbul, n.d., p. 181.

102 Whatever may have been her attachments to Turkey, Jamilah accompanied her husband to the Arab countries and remained with him until her death in 1966. Khaldun was born in Baghdad in 1923, his sister Salwa in 1926. Interview with Khaldun al-Husri, October 4, 1967.

ish national state did not appear as a possibility in the early months of 1919. The author has been unable to obtain a complete response concerning the motivations upon which Sati' acted at this time. He has explained his decision simply by saying that he was an Arab and that when the Arabs separated from the Ottoman Empire, he had no choice but to join them.[103] This may be a justification after the fact. Yet, it may also be true that despite the depth of his ties to Istanbul and the way of life there, his alternatives were limited. The Ottoman Empire and the ideology of Ottomanism could be served no longer.

Most Arabs with advanced training, wherever their wartime loyalties may have rested, appear to have recognized that their future opportunities lay outside Turkey. Dankwart Rustow reports that 15 percent of the graduates of the Mülkiye Mektebi living in 1920 went to Syria or Iraq while 7 percent of the living graduates of the War College did the same.[104] Musa Alami, scion of an established Palestinian family who had served the Ottoman forces briefly during the war, noted that when he and his parents departed from Istanbul for Jaffa in January 1919, their small cargo boat was jammed with several hundred other

[103] Interview with Sati' al-Husri, September 28, 1966.

[104] "The Development of Parties in Turkey" in Joseph LaPalombara and Myron Weiner (eds.), *Political Parties and Political Development*, Princeton, 1966, p. 129; and his "The Military: Turkey" in Robert E. Ward and Dankwart A. Rustow (eds.), *Political Modernization in Japan and Turkey*, Princeton, 1968, p. 388. Rustow uses these statistics to show that the bulk of the Ottoman-trained leadership cadres remained to serve the new Turkey while the talent available to create new states in the Arab lands was more limited. Yet no matter how small this pool of talent may have been in comparison to that available for Turkey, it did represent practically all the living Arab graduates from the two institutions and indicates that al-Husri's departure from Istanbul was part of a general exodus of state-trained Arab civil and military officials.

"stranded" Arabs who were also leaving the former Ottoman capital and returning to the Arab territories.[105]

Perhaps then, as Ernest Dawn has suggested, "the failure of the Ottoman Empire in World War I left the dominant faction of the Arab *élite* with no alternative to Arabism."[106] It is likely that Sati' analyzed the situation in a similar manner, and while such analysis made his decision no less difficult, it probably made it necessary. Thus, in June of 1919 he left Istanbul and journeyed to Damascus to enlist in a new cause which demanded a new ideology. His involvement in that cause and his contributions to that ideology transformed Sati' Bey the Ottoman into al-Husri the Arab nationalist.

[105] Geoffrey Furlonge, *Palestine Is My Country*, New York, 1969, p. 67.
[106] Dawn, "Rise of Arabism," p. 164.

CHAPTER

2

The Spokesman of Arab Nationalism, 1919–1968

First Involvement: Syria and its Aftermath, 1919–1921

The immediate post-war years in the Arab Middle East were filled with disillusioned hopes, confused negotiations, and armed revolt. Sati' al-Husri quickly became involved in the mainstream of these events and played a role of some importance in their unfolding. Thus, while a detailed discussion of the period will not be attempted here, a background summary must be presented.

When the Sharif of Mecca, Husayn ibn 'Ali, proclaimed the Arab revolt on the side of the Allies in June 1916, he felt that his long correspondence with the British High Commissioner in Cairo, Sir Henry McMahon, had resulted in a British promise to support the creation of an independent Arab state once hostilities had ceased.[1] The boundaries of

[1] For the Husayn-McMahon correspondence specifically and the conflicting interpretations given it, see Antonius, *Arab Awakening*, pp. 164-183; Appendix A; Zeine N. Zeine, *The Struggle for Arab Independence*, Beirut, 1960, pp. 6-10. A critical examination of the controversial agree-

the proposed state were ill-defined, and the motives of those who participated in the Arab revolt or joined the Arab cause after the armistice were frequently colored more by personal and local ambitions than by the concept of service to an abstract national idea. Nevertheless, Arab leaders generally accepted the British promise and looked forward to an independent existence and the future control of their own political destiny. But the exigencies of wartime diplomacy had prompted Great Britain into the contradictory Sykes-Picot agreement with her ally France. The terms of this secret agreement provided for the partition of the Ottoman Arab provinces into European spheres of influence. France would receive most of Lebanon and Syria, Britain would control Iraq, while Jerusalem and Palestine would be under international control.[2] Matters were further complicated by the Balfour Declaration of 1917 which committed Britain to a policy favoring the establishment of a Jewish homeland in Palestine.

With the end of the war, the contradictions inherent in these agreements burst forth with detrimental results for all parties. While Faysal pleaded his people's case at Versailles, France moved troops into Beirut, Great Britain consolidated her position in Iraq, and the Arabs in British-occupied Damascus grew impatient awaiting their independence. Finally, after protracted negotiations, Britain bowed to French demands for a more complete implementation of the Sykes-Picot agreement and withdrew her

---

ments of this period is also found in Tibawi, *Modern History of Syria*, chaps. VIII-X; and a good account of the interaction between Europe and the Middle East during the inter-war years is Elizabeth Monroe, *Britain's Moment in the Middle East, 1914-1956*, Baltimore, 1963.

2 The negotiations and terms of the agreement may be found in Antonius, *Arab Awakening*, pp. 243-253; Kedourie, *England and the Middle East*, pp. 29-66.

troops from Damascus and eastern Syria. At the same time, French forces in Lebanon and western Syria were strengthened as France prepared to insure her share of the agreement. She was given international sanction to do so by the San Remo Conference of April 1920 which awarded Britain the League of Nations mandate for Palestine and Iraq, and gave the mandate for Greater Syria (all of Syria and Lebanon) to France.[3]

Understandably bitter and disappointed, Arab nationalist leaders in Damascus were divided over the proper course of action in the face of what they regarded as Allied betrayal and duplicity. Should they submit to the mandate, hoping for the best, or should they prepare to resist with armed force?

In part, this division was caused by Faysal's frequent absences in Europe and the resulting lack of internal cohesion within the Arab leadership in Damascus. These brief but exciting months in the history of the new Arab movement awakened widespread feelings of Arab consciousness and attracted adherents representing a variety of backgrounds and interests. From Europe, from Cairo, from Istanbul and the Arab provinces of the Ottoman Empire came former CUP members and other officials, demobilized Arab soldiers and officers who had fought in the Ottoman armies as well as others who had been involved in the Arab revolt from its beginning. Prominent among these were such ex-Ottoman officers as Yasin and Taha al-Hashimi, Ja'far al-'Askari, Nuri al-Sa'id, and Yusuf al-'Azmah; domestic Syrian leaders like Hashim al-Atasi and Ihsan al-Jabiri; noted Lebanese like Riyad al-Sulh and Sa'id Haydar; and former Istanbul officials like Sati' al-Husri—all came to

[3] Zeine, *Struggle*, pp. 151-154.

Damascus and made that city truly "the *ka'abah* of every Arab patriot."[4]

An attempt was made to provide central leadership through the formation of a provisional government. Actual power, however, rested in the extra-governmental organizations, especially the influential *al-Fatat* and *Hizb al-istiqlal* (The Independence Party). These societies, in turn, were largely controlled by an element which soon became the dominant power group in Faysal's Syria—the Istanbul-trained Arab officers of the Ottoman army.[5] Thus, Yusuf al-'Azmah became Minister of War, Ja'far al-'Askari was Governor of Aleppo, Nuri al-Sa'id and Taha al-Hashimi operated near the center of civil and military power, and Yasin al-Hashimi served as Chief of Staff of the armed forces and was a leading voice in *al-Fatat*. With the notable exception of Yusuf al-'Azmah, officers of Iraqi origin were dominant in this group. One reason offered to explain the disproportionally large number of Istanbul-trained Iraqis in the Arab armed forces at this time is the pre-war practice of the Ottoman government of defraying all travel, food, lodging, and tuition expenses of Iraqi military students as a recruitment incentive. Such benefits were not given to students in the civil schools and the number of Iraqis grad-

[4] As'ad Daghir, *Mudhakkirati 'ala hamish al-qadiyyah al-'arabiyyah* (My Memoirs Concerning the Arab Question), Cairo, 1959, p. 106. See also Muhammad 'Izzat Darwazah, *Hawl al-harakah al-'arabiyyah al-hadithah* (On the Modern Arab Movement), I, Saidon, 1950, p. 71; Yusuf al-Hakim, *Suriyyah wa al-'ahd al-faysali* (Syria and the Era of Faysal), Beirut, 1966, p. 35; Amin Sa'id, *al-Thawrah al-'arabiyyah al-kubra* (The Great Arab Revolt), II, part I, Cairo, n.d. [1934], pp. 35-36, 66-67; Ahmad Qadri, *Mudhakkirati 'an al-thawrah al-'arabiyyah al-kubra* (My Memoirs on the Great Arab Revolt), Damascus, 1956, p. 130.

[5] Membership lists of these societies are found in Darwazah, *Harakah*, I, pp. 74-78; Sa'id, *al-Thawrah*, II, part I, pp. 35-37.

uating from them was correspondingly less.[6] Elie Kedourie probably overstates his case in calling these officers mere adventurers devoid of principle. But he is correct in suggesting that because of their Istanbul education and Ottoman training, they considered a leading place in the new power structure theirs by right.[7] This was true on all levels, even though a pre-war differential in rank had existed between lesser officers like Nuri al-Sa'id and a commander of Yasin al-Hashimi's stature and experience.

Sati' al-Husri was one of the late converts to Arab nationalism when he arrived in Damascus in July 1919. But when he made the cause of Arabism his own, he devoted all his considerable talents and energies to furthering that cause. Like most of the other high ranking Ottoman Arabs, his dominant position remained intact. This was true even though he was a civilian rather than a military figure. Darwazah states that al-Husri became a member of *al-Fatat*. Al-Husri has denied this, saying that although he was frequently taken into the counsels of various parties, he never joined any of them. He felt that Darwazah's statement probably resulted from Kurd 'Ali's claims.[8]

Nevertheless, al-Husri's educational activities had brought him maximum exposure in Istanbul and he was well known by most of the Arabs who had studied in the Ottoman capi-

6 Al-Husri, *al-Bilad al-'arabiyyah wa al-dawlah al-'uthmaniyyah*, pp. 84-86; and his *Mudhakkirati*, I, pp. 121-122.

7 Kedourie, *England and the Middle East*, p. 159; and the same author's "The Kingdom of Iraq," *The Chatham House Version and Other Middle Eastern Studies*, London, 1970, p. 271. Cf. the statistics given by R. Bayly Winder in "Syrian Deputies and Cabinet Ministers, 1919-1959," *The Middle East Journal*, XVI, no. 4 (1962), pp. 407-429; XVII, nos. 1-2 (1963), pp. 35-54.

8 Darwazah, *Harakah*, I, p. 77. Al-Husri's explanation is in *Questionnaire*, p. 20. See above, p. 43, for Kurd 'Ali's statements.

tal. Several, among them Nuri al-Sa'id, told al-Husri that they remembered attending some of his lectures before the war. Another, Talib Mushtaq, recalled how the *kaymakam* of his district in Iraq had distributed copies of *Tedrisat-i İptidaiye Mecmuasi* to advanced elementary students in his class and also remembered studying some of al-Husri's books on the natural sciences in a Baghdad secondary school.[9] When this author asked al-Husri how he made his initial contacts and introductions in Damascus, he replied in part, "When I went to Syria, there was no need to introduce me to anyone because my essays and lectures were known in all the Ottoman territories."[10]

In view of his reputation, therefore, al-Husri was made Director General of Education in the provisional government, and then served as Minister of Education in the two cabinets which were formed in independent Syria before the battle of Maysalun.[11] As he was to do in the same capital a quarter of a century later, al-Husri attempted to Arabize an educational system which had been controlled from the outside. He established a council of teaching and education to reintroduce systematically the use of Arabic in all the schools.[12]

But it was a period devoted more to a concern for Syria's very survival than to long-term education projects, and al-Husri, for one of the few times in his life, was deeply involved in day-to-day politics. Of significance in this context was the friendship he established with Faysal. The relationship between the two men was one of mutual respect and affection, and al-Husri became a trusted con-

[9] Interview with Sati' al-Husri, September 28, 1966; Talib Mushtaq, *Awraq ayyami* (The Pages of My Life), I, Beirut, 1968, pp. 28, 127.

[10] Al-Husri, *Questionnaire*, p. 20.

[11] Sa'id, *al-Thawrah*, II, part I, pp. 134, 145.

[12] Al-Husri, *Khulasah*, p. 6.

fidant. He has described in glowing terms his first meeting with the then Amir and the development of their relationship:

> I first met him in Damascus shortly after his return from the Peace Conference in Paris. . . . The relationship which began between the two of us that night was destined to continue and grow stronger without interruption for a period of over fourteen years during which I remained at his side and worked in his company until the last days of his life. . . . I accompanied him in the most critical circumstances of his life and the most magnificent days of his success. . . . During these years, I learned that he was great in every sense of the word.[13]

Meanwhile, the international and domestic problems of Syria were becoming more serious. In December 1919, the British troops left the area and were installed in Iraq. From that point on, lawlessness and disorder spread in Syria and spilled over the ill-defined border into Iraq where a bloody revolt against the British continued from June to October 1920, taking many lives on both sides and leaving lasting traces of hostility. Moral and material assistance was given to this outbreak by the Iraqi officers in Syria.[14] Nationalist agitation and a desire for self-assertion against the anticipated French move became such that the Syrian Congress declared independence and Faysal let himself be crowned King of Greater Syria in March 1920. Less than a month later the San Remo Conference was held and reports soon began to be received in Damascus concerning the massing of French troops in western Syria.

On July 14, 1920, the commander of the French forces, General Gouraud, dispatched an ultimatum to the Syrian Government demanding demobilization and recognition of

13 Al-Husri, *Safahat min al-madi al-qarib*, pp. 9-11.

14 See Philip W. Ireland, *Iraq*, London, 1937, pp. 266-276; Kedourie, *England and the Middle East*, p. 182; Zeine, *Struggle*, p. 146.

the mandate.[15] Whereas six months earlier Yasin al-Hashimi and Yusuf al-'Azmah, the Arab military commanders, had expressed confidence in the outcome of a military engagement with the French, they now admitted that they stood little chance.[16] Faysal and the cabinet reluctantly accepted the ultimatum on the day of the deadline. Yet the next day word came that the French had advanced toward Damascus. General Gouraud had not received Faysal's acceptance within the stipulated deadline because of cut telegraph lines. It was decided to dispatch a member of the government to Gouraud's headquarters in 'Alayh in order to reach an understanding with him on the matter. To his apparent surprise, al-Husri was chosen for the important task. He wrote in his diary, "I do not know why my colleagues immediately decided that the responsibility for this mission should be entrusted to me."[17] It was probably because of his excellent French. The hope that his civilian status might create a favorable impression with Gouraud could also have been a factor.

On the afternoon of July 21, al-Husri, accompanied by Jamil al-Ulashi, a former representative of Faysal's in Beirut, and Colonel Toulat, a French officer, left Damascus on this delicate mission. Delayed by troop movements, he did not reach 'Alayh until the next morning when he was quickly ushered into General Gouraud's headquarters. In the course of their negotiations, Gouraud asked for new guarantees which al-Husri did not feel empowered to give before consulting Faysal and the cabinet.[18] Accordingly, he

[15] The ultimatum is discussed in detail in Zeine, *Struggle*, pp. 164-174.

[16] Al-Husri, *Yawm Maysalun*, pp. 111-112, 122-123.

[17] *Ibid.*, p. 129.

[18] The details of these negotiations are given in *ibid.*, pp. 135-145.

returned to Damascus that night where he presented the General's new demands.

Acceptance would have met with resistance in the aroused Arab capital, and the government simply failed to act on the demands by the time the deadline expired. So, on the morning of July 24, 1920, French and Arab troops engaged in the uneven skirmish known as the Battle of Maysalun. It was over by noon. Arab troops scattered, Yusuf al-'Azmah was killed, and the government evacuated Damascus as the French moved in and established the mandate. Arab independence, which had been encouraged by the West, was now after barely five months of tortuous existence, efficiently terminated by the Troupes Françaises du Levant. Those Arabs who had served this ideal of independence were not likely to have faith in Western promises again.

Al-Husri, for his part, was now totally committed to the Arab cause as represented by Faysal and was unwilling or unable (Ülken says he was sentenced to death in absentia by the mandate authorities)[19] to remain in Syria and work under the French. After his departure from Damascus, he spent the next year in almost constant travel, much of it in the company of Faysal.[20] They became quite close during this period, the two outcasts with no country seeking support for a cause whose adherents had been dispersed from Amman and Cairo to Rome and Paris by Western occupation. What al-Husri wrote of Faysal at this time was applicable to himself as well: he was "leaving a life filled with achievements and memories in search of a new life in which were included a variety of possibilities."[21]

19 Ülken, *Tarihi,* I, p. 272.

20 This period in al-Husri's life is described in *Yawm Maysalun,* pp. 175-205.

21 Al-Husri, *Safahat min al-madi al-qarib,* p. 11.

They made their way under British protection from Syria to Port Said, and then embarked for Rome. Immediately upon arriving in Naples, however, al-Husri, because of his many Turkish contacts, was sent back to Istanbul to inquire about the possibility of support from the Kemalists against the French. When three weeks of discussions in Turkey proved fruitless, he returned to Italy where he met with Faysal at Lake Como, and then journeyed to Rome. From October to December 1920 al-Husri, at times incapacitated by illness, remained in Rome with his wife, writing letters to Istanbul explaining and defending the Arab cause and attempting to gain information about French and British plans for the Arab lands through the Italian Foreign Ministry.

The nature of al-Husri's private thoughts at this time is not known. He appeared to be committed to the Arab cause and did not use his visit to Istanbul to inquire about the possibility of returning. One of the letters which he wrote from Rome does, however, provide some indication of an effort on his part to rationalize the Arab situation and his own involvement with it. Dated October 29, 1920, the letter was intended for Yunus Nadi, an old Istanbul friend and the post-war editor of the Turkish newspaper *Yeni Gün* (The New Day). In his message, al-Husri refuted the charge that the Arab revolt against the Ottoman Empire had weakened the Muslim world and allowed it to be invaded by the West. He then went on to say that the revolt actually played no part at all in the final defeat of Germany and the Ottoman Empire. At one point he wrote:

> Is it possible that the course of the war was changed by the outbreak of the revolt in the Hejaz? Or that it would have been changed if there had been no revolt? Did this revolt possess the power and influence sufficient to bring about the defeat of

> Germany? I do not believe the revolt was of such significance. . . . The defeat and surrender of Germany were inevitable according to world conditions whether or not the revolt took place. So, too, was the collapse of the Ottoman Empire certain to occur following Germany's defeat, whether or not Sharif Husayn revolted against it.[22]

But what must be realized, continued al-Husri, is that the very fact of the revolt, of the existence of an Arab army in Syria, established the idea of Arab independence and produced a natural hostility when that independence was forcibly destroyed. In this manner the revolt, minor as it was on the stage of world power transformations, served to awaken the national feelings of the Arabs.[23] This letter may be an explanation for a course of action taken after the event. If the Arab revolt was irrelevant to the outcome of the war, al-Husri's decision not to participate in it was partially justified. At the same time, al-Husri showed himself not to have been disloyal to the Ottoman Empire. Furthermore, this letter presented an argument which made the imperialist powers rather than the Ottoman Empire appear to have been the object of the revolt. Al-Husri concluded by asking Yunus Nadi to forget his previous attitude toward the Arab revolt and to plan for a future of cooperation with the Arabs.

By this time, al-Husri was aware that the British were considering the possibility of installing Faysal as king of Iraq, and he felt that he could be of use there. He therefore left Italy and journeyed to Cairo where he awaited further word from Faysal. While in Cairo, he declined the offers of those exiles from Syria who urged him to join their struggle

22 Al-Husri, *Yawm Maysalun*, p. 190.

23 *Ibid.*, pp. 191-193. Part of this letter is reproduced in al-Husri, *Nushu' al-fikrah al-qawmiyyah*, pp. 221-224.

in Amman and others who asked him to return to Europe and participate in a propaganda campaign against the foreign occupation of the Arab territories.[24]

Within Iraq, Faysal's candidacy was opposed by certain local leaders, but encouraged by the repatriated Iraqi officers who had fled Syria and were gradually returning to Iraq from Egypt.[25] Great Britain, after some hesitation, decided that Faysal's selection could best rehabilitate her image among the Arabs and moderate the forces of Iraqi insurrection. After the agreement was reached, Faysal passed through Cairo and told al-Husri that he would be invited to serve in the Iraqi educational system as soon as possible.

While Faysal spent two months in Hejaz, al-Husri busied himself in Cairo learning about Iraq. He did not know very much about the country and studied its ancient history and talked to men who had participated in the recent revolts there. In addition, he was granted permission to visit certain Egyptian schools in order to study the methods of instruction in what he felt was the most Arabized educational system in the Middle East.[26] Yet, the Egyptian attitude toward Arabism troubled al-Husri and occupied a major portion of his writings in the years to come.

He had been in Cairo briefly in 1919, his visit coinciding with the revolt against the British. Deeply moved by the spirit of patriotism and sacrifice which he witnessed at that time, al-Husri believed that the Egyptians were bound to

24 Al-Husri, *Yawm Maysalun*, p. 204.

25 Ireland, *Iraq*, p. 289. See also pp. 303-326 in Ireland's work for a discussion of the negotiations leading to Faysal's accession. The intense nature of the opposition to Faysal in Iraq is treated in Kedourie, "The Kingdom of Iraq," *Chatham House Version*, pp. 236-282.

26 Al-Husri, *Mudhakkirati*, I, p. 22.

the rest of the Arab world by feelings of Arabism and opposition to foreign rule.[27] He was thus profoundly affected by Egypt's apparent disavowal of Arabism and her lack of concern over the French occupation of Syria. For the next forty years, al-Husri wrote article after article urging the Egyptians to assume their destined role in the Arab nationalist movement.[28]

While al-Husri was analyzing these problems, he received a telegram in July 1921 asking him to come to Baghdad immediately. The night before his departure from Port Said, he stayed in the same hotel where he, Faysal, and Nuri al-Sa'id had stayed the year before, after their flight from Damascus. Only this time, he wrote that instead of going west, he was going east to begin a new page in his life.[29]

Institutionalizing Nationalism: Iraq, 1921–1941

This troubled period of Iraqi history in which al-Husri participated will not be recorded in detail.[30] The inhabitants of the mandated territory which was created from the former Ottoman vilayets of Baghdad, Mosul, and Basra were not universally receptive either to the British or to

[27] Al-Husri, *Ara' wa ahadith fi al-qawmiyyah al-'arabiyyah* (Views and Discussions on Arab Nationalism), 4th ed., Beirut, 1964, pp. 15-16. Hereafter *al-Qawmiyyah al-'arabiyyah.*

[28] See below, pp. 132-138.

[29] Al-Husri, *Mudhakkirati*, I, p. 22.

[30] Factual accounts may be found in Ireland, *Iraq*, chaps. 15-23; Majid Khadduri, *Independent Iraq, 1932-1958*, 2nd ed. rev., London, 1960; Stephen H. Longrigg, *Iraq, 1900-1950*, London, 1953. The most detailed treatment of political affairs is the work by 'Abd al-Razzaq al-Hasani, *Ta'rikh al-wizarat al-'iraqiyyah* (The History of Iraqi Ministries), 1st ed., 10 vols., Saidon, 1933-1961. Examples of the factional characteristics of Iraqi politics are illustrated in Kedourie, "The Kingdom of Iraq," *Chatham House Version*, pp. 237-239, 250-254.

their new king from Hejaz. With a bitter Shi'ite majority almost totally unrepresented in the state political power structure, with a large Jewish community in a similar position, and with competing tribal forces unreconciled to the imposition of centralized government control, Iraq was a volatile and divided entity.

As had happened in Syria, the coterie of Istanbul-trained Iraqi officers quickly assumed a dominant position in the political life of the country, regularly exchanging the office of Prime Minister and various cabinet posts.[31] Their assumption of power and their methods of exercising it further alienated the disaffected elements of the population. When Iraq received independence and admission to the League of Nations in 1932, the country had achieved only the most fragile balance of its conflicting forces under Faysal's rule. After his death a year later, personal jealousies, the absence of forceful leadership from his son, King Ghazi, and other centrifugal tendencies combined to cause the further division of the ex-Ottoman elite and to inject additional chaos into the already unstable political system.

Furthermore, this elite's monopoly of political power began to be challenged by a younger generation, imbued with the ideas of Arab nationalism as taught in the Iraqi school system, who demanded a chance to participate in the

[31] For example, in the 28 cabinets formed between September 1921 and the Rashid 'Ali coup d'état in April 1941, the office of Prime Minister was held five times by Nuri al-Sa'id, four times by Jamil Midfa'i, twice by Ja'far al-'Askari and Yasin al-Hashimi, and once by Taha al-Hashimi and 'Ali Jawdat. All had received military training in Istanbul. See the lists in Khadduri, *Independent Iraq*, pp. 370-371; and the information on educational background in al-Husri, *Mudhakkirati*, II, pp. 558-559. See also, Kedourie, "Pan-Arabism and British Policy," *Chatham House Version*, pp. 213-214, for a condemnation of the political behavior of these officers.

political life of the nation.[32] As the quarreling factions sought alliances, the army emerged as the effective arbiter of Iraqi politics, and a more vocal nationalist policy was voiced by the ministers under its control.[33] Yet the army itself was composed of shifting power blocs, and the first coup, led by Bakr Sidqi in 1936, was followed by several more which culminated in the Rashid 'Ali government of 1941.

Throughout this period, al-Husri avoided active participation in politics. A partial explanation for this action rests with Faysal's determination to provide continuity in the Iraqi educational system by attempting to secure al-Husri's permanent appointment as Director General of Education.[34] He was, in effect, given immunity to the rise and fall of governments, retaining his powerful position while Ministers of Education were replaced and then reappointed in the fluctuating political life of the country. Furthermore, al-Husri himself believed that his participation in party politics would jeopardize his usefulness to education. He viewed politics as having two functional divisions. What he termed "secondary politics" was influenced by party positions and the changes of officials and ministers, changes which were often based on personality considerations. By its very nature such politics caused confusion and was best kept from the classroom.[35]

[32] See the editor's introduction in Taha al-Hashimi, *Mudhakkirat Taha al-Hashimi, 1919-1943* (The Memoirs of Taha al-Hashimi), Khaldun al-Husri (ed.), Beirut, 1967.

[33] For details on the army's involvement in Iraqi politics, see Khadduri, *Independent Iraq*, pp. 68-211; Longrigg, *Iraq*, pp. 247-297.

[34] Al-Husri, *Mudhakkirati*, I, pp. 136-137, 246, 263-265.

[35] Al-Husri, *Ara' wa ahadith fi al-tarbiyah wa al-ta'lim* (Views and Discussions on Pedagogy and Education), Cairo, 1944, p. 148. Hereafter, cited *al-Tarbiyah wa al-ta'lim*.

There also existed a higher politics, however, which was concerned with the achievement of fundamental national goals, among them the fostering of patriotism and nationalism.[36] Al-Husri quite consciously equated his efforts with this plane of politics. In his memoirs he recorded his decision by writing: "I will employ every means to strengthen the feelings of nationalism among the sons of Iraq and to spread a belief in the unity of the Arab nation. And I shall do this without joining any of the political parties which will eventually be formed."[37]

On the surface, then, al-Husri's career in Iraq appears to parallel his Ottoman activities: he was an innovating, aggressive educator, especially during his tenure as Director General of Education (1923–1927), and has been termed the father of public instruction in Iraq;[38] he remained deeply concerned with the standard of instruction, participating in the reorganization of Dar al-Mu'allimin, teaching in that institution for four years, and founding and editing *Majallah al-tarbiyah wa al-ta'lim* (The Journal of Pedagogy and Education) which had objectives similar to those of *Tedrisat-i İptidaiye*; and outside the sphere of his official activities he was a noted lecturer and author on the need to generate vitality within the society.[39]

Yet, there was a significant difference in the ultimate

36 *Ibid.*, p. 148; al-Husri, *Mudhakkirati*, I, pp. 37-38.

37 Al-Husri, *Mudhakkirati*, I, p. 38; II, p. 525. A recent Arab biography attests to al-Husri's success in avoiding political involvement. See Burj, *al-Husri*, p. 211.

38 'Ajjan al-Hadid [Robert Montagne], "Le Développement de l'éducation nationale en Iraq," *Revue des Études Islamiques*, no. 3 (1932), p. 236.

39 For these activities, see al-Husri, *Mudhakkirati*, I, pp. 201-210, 348-349. He edited *Majallah al-tarbiyah wa al-ta'lim* from 1928 to 1932. A brief analysis of the first five issues, nos. 1-5 (January-May 1928), can be found in *Revue des Études Islamiques*, no. 2 (1928), pp. 177-178.

intellectual objectives of the two careers of Sati' al-Husri. Whereas Sati' Bey the Ottoman had envisaged a broad-based system of loyalties in which there would be ample scope for the existence of a variety of languages, cultures, and individual responses, al-Husri the Arab nationalist sought the assimilation of diverse elements of the population into a homogeneous whole tied by the bonds of specific language, history, and culture to a comprehensive but still exclusive ideology of Arabism.

This latter goal was reflected in his educational policies which limited the scope of individual initiative and provided a coherent, controlled national ideology throughout the school system. For example, the new elementary school curriculum which he introduced in 1923 was focused inward: it delayed English language training until a year later than had been usual; it arranged that the history of other nations should be studied in the early courses only as it related to Arab history; and it stipulated that the history of Iraq and the Arabs was to be taught in a manner which would strengthen nationalistic sentiments among the students.[40]

The obvious nationalistic orientation of this system did not hinder al-Husri's intention to improve the overall quality of education in both the sciences and the humanities. A pedagogical professionalism dominated even his nationalist approach to education. He objected always to the lowering of educational standards by overzealous nationalists such as Sami Shawkat, and in private often called them charlatans.[41] This attitude is illustrated by his reaction to

[40] Al-Husri, *Mudhakkirati*, I, pp. 212-215. The curriculum is reproduced on p. 212. See also pp. 479-480; II, p. 340.

[41] Letter from Khaldun al-Husri, August 1, 1969. Shawkat served as Director General of Education in 1933 and 1939 and also headed the Futuwwah paramilitary youth organization.

Shawkat's famous speech, "The Profession of Death."[42] Although al-Husri valued Shawkat's objectives insofar as they were directed toward sacrifice in the cause of the fatherland, there was a point beyond which he would not go. When Shawkat called for the excavation of Ibn Khaldun's grave and the burning of his books on the grounds that they contained passages which were critical of the Arabs, al-Husri retorted that "this was blind fanaticism before which it was impossible to remain silent. Such a call was incompatible with the requirements both of patriotism and of true pedagogical principles."[43]

To meet these two requirements, al-Husri demanded teachers of the highest caliber. Not only did he deplore the intellectual heresy of Shawkat, but he also sharply criticized the traditional religious instructors with their limited knowledge and abilities and did not hesitate, although it cost him dearly in criticism, to bring in qualified Arab teachers from outside Iraq.[44] While he professed to favor a system granting a large measure of initiative to the district supervisors on the Ottoman model, he in fact kept the organization tightly controlled, constantly issuing detailed directives which ranged from curriculum changes to the proper form to be used in submitting reports to his office.[45]

[42] The speech was delivered in Baghdad in 1933 and is reproduced in part in Haim, *Arab Nationalism*, pp. 97-99.

[43] Al-Husri, *Mudhakkirati*, II, pp. 160-161.

[44] Al-Husri, *Mudhakkirati*, I, pp. 323-325; Mushtaq, *Ayyami*, pp. 123-126; Amin al-Rihani, *Muluk al-'arab* (The Kings of the Arabs), II, 2nd ed., Beirut, 1929, p. 402. Cf. Matta Akrawi, "The Arab World" in *The Year Book of Education, 1949*, London, 1949, p. 433.

[45] This concentration of power at the top was later criticized by an American Commission of Educational Inquiry. The Commission, headed by Paul Monroe of Columbia University, noted in 1932 that the most important characteristic of the Iraqi educational system was the complete centralization of its administration and suggested that such rigid

Even though subject to frequent criticisms, the effect of these policies, as long as they were directed by al-Husri, was to raise both the general level of Iraqi education and the nationalistic tenor of the country to a considerable degree.[46]

Yet despite his many contributions to the country and his own self-identification as an Arab, al-Husri occupied an ambivalent position in Iraq. A Syrian among Iraqis, a graduate of the Mülkiye among individuals with military and traditional training, a cosmopolitan, French-speaking intellectual and administrator among tribal shaykhs, local religious leaders, and officers turned politicians, he never completely belonged. Even Arabic, to which he attached such importance in his nationalist ideology, was a third language to him. Although he learned to express himself clearly in print and became an effective public speaker, he

---

central control inhibited individual initiative and community participation. While al-Husri denied the restrictive results of centralization, the findings of the Monroe Commission do provide evidence that the basic educational structure which al-Husri established as Director General was firmly controlled from the top and was based on the premise that curriculum uniformity could create a sense of national identity. See Paul Monroe (ed.), *Report of the Educational Inquiry Commission*, Baghdad, 1932, esp. pp. 7-9. Al-Husri's reply to the Commission is contained in his *Naqd taqrir lajnah Monroe* (A Criticism of the Report of the Monroe Commission), Baghdad, 1932. He has also included a detailed summary in *Mudhakkirati*, II, pp. 165-255. A statement on the powerful position into which al-Husri built the Director Generalship of Education and summaries of the Commission's report and al-Husri's defense may also be found in Hadid, "Le Développement de l'éducation nationale," pp. 236-257.

[46] Al-Husri was apparently able to operate with a certain degree of independence from the British mandate authorities. Great Britain's *Report to the League of Nations* mentions that in the substitution of Iraqi for British control, the Ministry of Education was ahead of all other departments. *Special Report . . . on the Progress of Iraq during the Period 1920-1931*, London, 1931, p. 224.

retained a heavy Turkish accent.[47] As described in the following passage by Amin al-Rihani, al-Husri's general style of life was somewhat unique in inter-war Iraq:

> Sati' was one of the specialists in education. . . . It does not matter that he was born in Syria (*sic*) and not Iraq; he is an Arab, irreproachable in his Arabism except for his accent . . . and he is one of those few who have liberated themselves and their homes from the bonds of social traditions. I think that his sitting room is the only one in Baghdad in which the lady of the house receives visitors unveiled and participates with them in the conversation.[48]

Furthermore, al-Husri's methods of administration engendered a certain hostility toward him within his adopted country. Operating on a set of modern Western theories and practices and accustomed to a position of authority in educational matters, he was quick to criticize those who failed to understand and carry out his requests for change.

His memoirs of this period present a picture of him descending upon teachers, school directors, religious instructors, and British advisers with his rapid-fire critical questions, his blunt comments, and his uncompromising recommendations for reforms.[49] By seeking to impose a unified, state-controlled system of education disseminating doctrines of pan-Arabism in a country as deeply rent by political, sectarian, and tribal differences as Iraq, al-Husri,

[47] Interview with Khaldun al-Husri, April 12, 1967. Khaldun told the author that their house in Baghdad had books and magazines in Turkish, Arabic, English, and French and that he grew up with a certain knowledge of them all. As soon as he began school, however, Arabic became his principal language.

[48] Al-Rihani, *Muluk al-'arab*, II, p. 402. See also the same author's *Qalb al-'Iraq* (The Heart of Iraq), 2nd ed. rev., Beirut, 1957, p. 221.

[49] See, for example, the description of his initial organizational activities at the Ministry of Education in al-Husri, *Mudhakkirati*, I, pp. 105-155.

even had he been more tactful, would have aroused antagonisms. But he refused to cater to communal fears and persistently pushed through his program of national assimilation, opposing the opening of teacher training colleges when he felt sectarian sentiments would dominate them, restricting the financial and curricular autonomy of foreign-sponsored schools, rejecting the concept of a distinction between the rural and urban systems, especially on the matter of special schools for bedouins, and conducting a general attack on Shi'ite educational institutions and methods.[50]

His administrative conduct produced embittered hostility from some quarters and deep loyalty from others. An Egyptian writer noted with alarm the spread of Husrism (*al-husriyyah*) in Iraq in the 1920s and 1930s, charging that its stand toward non-Arab elements made it ultimately a divisive and harmful doctrine.[51] Yet one of the Director General's young supporters, Talib Mushtaq, compared him to the generic group of isolated reformers everywhere who become the objects of fabricated rumors and slanderous assaults from those who shrink from progressive change. He identified al-Husri's enemies as the incompetent fearing dismissal, the religious fanatics opposed to secularization, the envious, and the greedy.[52]

Al Husri's political immunity created further problems

[50] These attitudes and programs are found in *ibid.*, I, pp. 79-80, 147-155, 163-175, 311-319; II, 300-303. A critical evaluation of al-Husri's policies in this regard is contained in Kedourie, "The Kingdom of Iraq," *Chatham House Version*, pp. 273-275.

[51] Kedourie, "The Kingdom of Iraq," *Chatham House Version*, p. 274.

[52] Mushtaq, *Ayyami*, pp. 129-130; cf. Burj, *al-Husri*, pp. 48-49. Talib Mushtaq (b. 1900) worked in the Iraqi Ministry of Education from 1921 to 1931, expressing the highest regard for al-Husri's methods and principles. He later held several foreign service posts and served as Director of the Arab Bank in Baghdad.

and embroiled him in a continuous series of controversies with the Ministers of Education under whom he served as Director General. This tension was first of all a result of the failure to differentiate the spheres of authority between al-Husri and the Ministers. Al-Husri felt that he was the expert and wanted the ultimate decision-making power, while the Ministers, in turn, wished to assert the rights of their office. The tension was deepened by the fact that the Ministers of Education were the only Shi'ite members of the cabinet, appointed for their potential to placate communal and sectarian feelings rather than for their educational expertise, and automatically intolerable to al-Husri for these very reasons.[53] He ignored them or tried to circumvent them to the point where a Shi'ite proclamation of 1932 complained that the Shi'ite portfolio of education carried "little, if any, power or prestige."[54]

Moreover, the stubborn and inflexible nature of his personality antagonized many of the people with whom he had to deal and served further to isolate him. He acted according to the dictates of strict rational principles and possessed little tolerance for human frailties. The complex of political and personal interests affected by some of his recommendations often went unrecognized by him. Although known and respected throughout Iraq, his cold intellectuality provided him with few friends. His most intimate acquaintances had been left behind in Istanbul and, while he was deeply devoted to Faysal and got along well with Yasin al-Hashimi,

[53] Examples of the friction are found in al-Husri, *Mudhakkirati*, I, pp. 272-273, 279-294. The confessional nature of the appointment of Education Ministers is briefly treated in Hadid, "Le Développement de l'éducation nationale," p. 236; and al-Rihani, *Qalb al-'Iraq*, p. 221.

[54] The proclamation is reproduced in Kedourie, "The Kingdom of Iraq," *Chatham House Version*, pp. 283-285; the quotation is from p. 284.

he felt closest to Rustum Haydar who was himself an expatriate civilian of European education and culture.[55]

Even al-Husri's espousal of a broad Arab nationalism, which was at once cause and effect of his socio-political ambivalence, tended to reflect a personal struggle for identity as well as a reasoned and appealing program.[56] Both his educational philosophy and his broader nationalist doctrines were designed to formulate an ideology which would inspire allegiance to national above regional bonds and to create an immediate sense of communal identity among the inhabitants of the divided post-war Arab nation. Yet, in urging an inclusive national self-awareness among the Arabs, al-Husri may also have been formulating a frame of reference with which he, himself, could identify. Obviously, when he introduced the concept of nation into his ideology, he demanded from himself and from his audience a more specific sense of loyalty based on more limited bonds than he had done in his Ottoman *Vatan İçin* lectures.

[55] Interview with Khaldun al-Husri, September 12, 1967; al-Husri, *Mudhakkirati*, II, pp. 525-526. Haydar was from Ba'albek in Lebanon and was educated at the Mülkiye and the Sorbonne. He became Faysal's personal secretary and held several cabinet positions until his murder in 1940. See al-Yafi, *al-'Iraq bayn inqilabayn*, pp. 111-113; Khadduri, *Independent Iraq*, pp. 149-152.

[56] The present author possesses neither the type of information on al-Husri nor the professional knowledge required to present a psychological study like the one contained in Erik Erikson's brilliant *Young Man Luther*, New York, 1962. The term identity is used in our discussion to indicate the orientation of one's political and societal loyalties, the ideological frame of reference within which a person views himself. Erikson's study, although it is basically concerned with the psychological development of an adolescent to young manhood, does not neglect the interaction of personality with ideology. See esp., pp. 41-42, 176-182. For a study of the conflicts of identity and ideology within one person in an Arab setting, see Elie Kedourie, "Religion and Politics," *Chatham House Version*, pp. 317-342.

In this sense al-Husri applied in an Arab setting arguments similar to those used by Ziya Gökalp during the latter's efforts to define Turkish nationality. Nevertheless, by refusing to place himself solely within a Syrian or Iraqi context and choosing instead to identify with the larger Arab nation, al-Husri remained to some extent within his Ottoman tradition. This does not deny a possible internal conflict which posited a very definite choice in his mind between remaining in Istanbul and joining the Arabs; it suggests instead that having selected Arabism, al-Husri was naturally led to an intellectual effort to justify his selection, and that a continuing and vocal commitment toward shaping the cause he had chosen was demanded of him. In fact, al-Husri and Yasin al-Hashimi were often accused by their Iraqi contemporaries of practicing an overzealous nationalism in an attempt to compensate for their nonparticipation in the Arab cause prior to the end of World War I.[57]

Despite these problems, it is unquestionable that al-Husri was sincere in his ultimate articulation of Arabism and the projection of his own Arabness. The intense nature of this projection is represented repeatedly in his works by such passages as the following: "I am an Arab to the core and I profess the religion of Arabism with all my heart. . . ."[58] It

[57] Interview with Khaldun al-Husri, October 4, 1967. Cf. Kedourie, "The Kingdom of Iraq," *Chatham House Version*, p. 277, for an analysis of the criticism levelled at Yasin by Nuri al-Sa'id and Ja'afar al-'Askari upon the occasion of Yasin's opposition to the Iraqi-British treaty of 1931 which Nuri had negotiated.

[58] Al-Husri, "Naqd nizam al-ta'lim fi Misr" (A Critique of the System of Education in Egypt), in *al-Tarbiyah wa al-ta'lim*, p. 184. This essay originally appeared in the journal *al-Risalah*, v, no. 187 (1937). Vigorous statements on al-Husri's total involvement in the Arab cause are provided in Burj, *al-Husri*, pp. 91-92, 101-103, and in 'Adnan al-Khatib, "Faqid al-'urubah" (The Deceased of Arabism), *Majallah majma' al-lughah al-'arabiyyah fi Dimashq*, XLIV, no. 3 (1969), p. 447.

can be suggested, however, that al-Husri demonstrated an intellectual capacity to select applicable doctrines for a specific situation from a broad range of understood alternatives (it will be remembered that he recognized but refrained from espousing nationalist concepts for several years prior to 1919) and so worked from an intellectual to an emotional position rather than the reverse.

Al-Husri was, then, somewhat on the margin of Arab society.[59] Yet, this marginality led not to detachment, but rather to an intense endeavor to come to terms with the process in which he was participant and initiator. Educator, journalist, antiquities director, and nationalist ideologue, as well as author of essays on sociology, anthropology, biology, mathematics, linguistics, literature, and history, al-Husri performed a variety of functions after he joined the Arabs. But despite the apparent dispersion of his activities, he attempted to channel them all into a single serviceable focus—the propagation of Arab nationalism. Simultaneously, al-Husri was provided, because of his marginality, with a nonlocalized view of this process. As an intellectual and an outsider, he was well placed to analyze the total Arab situation, to ask questions and propose solutions which cut across local loyalties and political interests and quite naturally involved him in disputes.

Already by 1927 opposition to him was such that his position as Director General of Education became intolerable. Al-Husri identified his critics as those whose self-interests ran contrary to his direct methods of improving educational content and administration; but he also recognized that a prolonged controversy would paralyze the

59 A similar observation has been made by Hourani in *Arabic Thought*, pp. 311-312.

educational structure and perhaps embarrass those who supported him.[60] He therefore resigned.

For the next four years he taught at Dar al-Muʻallimin in Baghdad and continued to dominate Iraqi education through his publications and his active participation on several committees. Although some were relieved at al-Husri's departure from the center of administrative power, there were others in the Iraqi parliament who began to feel that a sharp decline became evident in the functioning of the educational system following his resignation. A new position was therefore created and al-Husri was persuaded to accept it. Once again the relentless reformer, his tenure as Inspector General of Education lasted only from October to December 1931.[61] His choice for Director General, Sami Shawkat, soon proved to be a disappointment and cooperation between the two men became impossible. Al-Husri responded in his usual manner to a situation which threatened to degenerate into political infighting by resigning.

He then assumed the position of Dean of the Law College and served in that capacity until 1935. It was by no means an isolated post and al-Husri's opinionated concern for the orientation of education embroiled him in a running series of disagreements with Shawkat and Fadil al-Jamali, an American-educated Iraqi who exercised considerable influence on education at this time. In addition to his Law College duties, al-Husri was appointed Director of Antiquities in 1934 and also served another stormy year in the Ministry of Education. From 1936 to 1941 he held the single position of Director of Antiquities. In part, his appointment in this capacity was used to remove him entirely from educational

60 Al-Husri, *Mudhakkirati,* I, pp. 611-615; II, pp. 113-114; Burj, *al-Husri,* p. 49.

61 On this period, see al-Husri, *Mudhakkirati,* II, pp. 111-139.

affairs where he had become the center of so much controversy. It was also felt that he could serve in creating a nationalistic interest in Iraqi antiquities while at the same time limiting the activities of European archeologists.[62]

Al-Husri brought boundless energy to this new post and demonstrated a rapid ability to learn. He even became respected enough in his field to be appointed by the League of Nations to its consultative commission of experts for art, archeology, and ethnology.[63] In the restoration of palaces and the establishment of a museum, he showed himself again to be an effective administrator when power was concentrated in his hands. As always, his efforts revolved around the establishment of pride in Arab history. So insistent was he on Iraq's right to obtain a more equitable allotment of the treasures unearthed by foreign expeditions that at one point he caused the cautious Nuri al-Sa'id considerable concern about the ramifications for Iraqi-American relations.[64]

During this period, al-Husri also continued his travels. He had already gone to Spain in 1926 and he visited Istanbul in 1931 and Cairo in 1935 and 1937. He also journeyed to Morocco, Algeria, and Tunisia in 1939 on a mission related to his work in antiquities. Upon his return he praised the natural beauty and the Arabness of these North African countries.[65]

Believing as he did in the need to expose as large an audience as possible to the nationalist ideology, al-Husri's activities were not confined to his official functions. Indeed, it

62 Interview with Khaldun al-Husri, October 4, 1967.

63 The letter of appointment is reproduced in al-Husri, *Mudhakkirati*, II, p. 450.

64 This incident is discussed in *ibid.*, II, pp. 417-423.

65 Al-Husri, "Shamal afriqiya wa al-'urubah" (North Africa and Arabism), *al-Risalah*, VIII, no. 339 (1940), p. 39.

can be suggested that a large part of his reputation was achieved elsewhere, in his lectures and articles dealing with Arab nationalism. From his position on the margin of society, he was able to expound a general Arab nationalist doctrine devoid of political and regional considerations. Again, he can be seen attempting to function on the plane of his own "higher politics."

For example, on the 1921 journey from Egypt to Iraq, al-Husri told a group of young officers that it was impossible to rely on the government for everything. The people of the country, especially the youth, should complement governmental activities by forming clubs and societies. A simple repetition of the exclusive Arab Club of Damascus was not enough; rather, the situation called for societies which comprised a broader membership and served a more extensive interest.[66] It was in such nationalist organizations as the Muthanna Club and the Cultural Club, in the lecture hall of Dar al-Mu'allimin, on the radio, and in numerous articles that al-Husri earned his reputation as one of the leading spokesmen of Arab nationalism.[67]

During the years 1936 to 1941, national agitation in Iraq increased to a considerable degree.[68] Baghdad had gradually replaced Damascus as the intellectual and political

[66] Al-Husri, *Mudhakkirati*, I, pp. 25-26.

[67] The Muthanna Club was founded in Baghdad in 1935 and became a center for the propagation of pan-Arabism. Al-Husri spoke at this club many times. See Khadduri, *Independent Iraq*, p. 166; Longrigg, *Iraq*, p. 273. The Cultural Club was the Iraqi branch of the League of Arab Culture established in 1931 to coordinate Arab cultural activities between Baghdad and Cairo. Al-Husri was one of the founders of the League and, although it never lived up to his expectations insofar as its inter-Arab functions were concerned, the Baghdad group was quite active. See al-Husri, *Mudhakkirati*, II, pp. 73-78.

[68] See Khaldun al-Husri's introduction in *Mudhakkirat Taha al-Hashimi* for a suggestive discussion of this period.

center of Arab nationalism, first because of the comparatively lenient policy of the British mandate authorities, and later because the achievement of independence and membership in the League of Nations gave Iraq unique prestige in the Arab world. To its capital came the discontented from Palestine and Syria, the professional agitators whose presence added to the tension in the country. Nationalist sentiments were further aroused by a series of Arab revolts against the British mandate and the Zionist presence in Palestine in the period 1936 to 1939. At the same time, increased German propaganda found a sympathetic reception among many Iraqis.

During these five years, al-Husri's involvement in nationalist activities became more pronounced. Neither flamboyant in the manner of Sami Shawkat nor overly militaristic like some of the young officers, he used impassioned but reasoned arguments in the cause of Arab unity and national solidarity. His advocacy of total Arab unity led him to disagree with Nuri al-Sa'id over the issue of Iraq's international loyalties. Nuri's Arab nationalism was predicated on a belief that Arab demands could best be met by means of a gradual accommodation with the British. During the decade following 1921, al-Husri also believed in the necessity of some cooperation with the British presence in order to consolidate the new Iraqi state. With the worsening of the international situation, however, al-Husri and others came to demand Iraqi neutrality and sought to exert leverage on the Western powers so as to obtain concessions for Palestine and Syria. Thus, while Nuri opposed sending arms to Palestine which would be used against British soldiers, al-Husri favored such shipments and objected to Nuri's attitude of total loyalty to Britain.[69]

[69] Letter from Khaldun al-Husri, August 1, 1969.

Al-Husri's reputation as an ardent nationalist was well established when the Rashid 'Ali al-Kaylani coup occurred in April 1941. Engineered by a powerful group of four army officers in combination with the politician, Rashid 'Ali, the coup was the result of a long series of disagreements with Britain over arms shipments and the continuing Western presence in Syria, nationalist frustration in the army over not being able to play as dynamic a role in aiding the Palestinian Arabs as it desired, internal political rivalries, and Iraq's desire to maintain her neutrality in the war.[70] The coup was not pro-Fascist in ideology so much as it was the interaction of nationalist forces within Iraq with the powers that seemed most likely to help them achieve their own particular aims without interfering once those goals were reached. Supporters of British policy in Iraq, among them Nuri al-Sa'id and 'Abd al-Ilah, the acting Regent for the young king, Ghazi II, fled the country while British forces invaded Iraq and quickly defeated the forces supporting Rashid 'Ali. The Regent and Nuri returned to power "under the protection of British bayonets," in al-Husri's phrase.[71]

The leaders of the coup were sentenced to death, many of their supporters were placed in prison camps, and several of the more outspoken nationalists were stripped of their Iraqi citizenship and ordered to leave the country.[72] One of these was Sati' al-Husri. Taha al-Hashimi reports

[70] In addition to the general histories of Iraq already mentioned, accounts of the Rashid 'Ali coup may be found in Lukasz Hirszowicz, *The Third Reich and the Arab East*, London, 1966, chaps. VI-VIII; George Kirk, *The Middle East in the War*, London, 1952, pp. 56-78.

[71] Al-Husri, *Khulasah*, p. 8.

[72] For details on the sentences and expulsions, see Muhammad al-Durrah, *al-Harb al-'iraqiyyah al-baritaniyyah, 1941* (The Iraqi-British War, 1941), Beirut, 1969, pp. 417-419.

that after he had confirmed the rumor about al-Husri's loss of citizenship, he informed his old acquaintance "who was calm on hearing the news."[73] Al-Husri himself regarded his actions as strictly in accordance with nationalist principles. In his memoirs, he wrote that one of his main purposes in Iraq had been to spread a belief in the unity of the Arab nation, and he then added: "I worked for this goal, sometimes directly and other times indirectly, within the sphere of my official capacities as well as outside them. . . . In summary, then, I took every opportunity and used every means to work in this cause. It is painful for me to say that this was the reason which prompted the government of 'Abd al-Ilah to expel me from Iraq and deprive me of my Iraqi citizenship in 1941."[74]

Al-Husri was immediately taken to the Iraqi-Syrian border at Kujik and on June 23 he was put on the train to Aleppo. Once again an exile, he felt he had been the victim of a government which had discarded the principle of Arabism in favor of collaboration with the British.

[73] Al-Hashimi, *Mudhakkirat Taha al-Hashimi*, pp. 456-457.

[74] Al-Husri, *Mudhakkirati*, I, p. 10. Officially, al-Husri was expelled on the basis of a decree which allowed the government to deprive of their citizenship persons who were not descended from families that had lived in Iraq before 1914. The decree was known as Mar Sham'un after the Assyrian religious leader and it was originally promulgated in order to expel the Assyrians from the country following their uprising in 1933. Al-Husri bitterly noted, "I had become harmful to the well-being of Iraq like Mar Sham'un!" See al-Husri, *Mudhakkirati*, II, pp. 519-521. His citizenship was restored by a unanimous vote of the Iraqi parliament in 1952.

A somewhat more spectacular, but undocumented, version of the event is given by Burj, *al-Husri*, p. 55, who hints at plots and treats the expulsion as a personal duel between two individuals, al-Husri and 'Abd al-Ilah, who publicly stood for different beliefs and therefore could not coexist in the same country.

The Senior Spokesman, 1941–1968

From Aleppo, al-Husri went to Beirut where he lived for three years. Then in 1944 he was invited by the newly independent Syrian government to serve in an advisory capacity during the reorganization of the educational system.[75] His principles and methods were the same as they had been in Iraq. Al-Husri termed the educational policies which had been practiced under the mandate "a slavish imitation of the French system" and he condemned the attempts to isolate Syria from the mainstream of Arab nationalism through the imposition of French language and culture.[76] He further argued that the elimination of the French mandate would not automatically eliminate the cultural influence implanted by that mandate. In his sixteen reports written between March and July 1944 and collected as *Taqarir 'an halat al-ma'arif fi Suriyyah wa iqtirahat li islahiha* (Reports on the Condition of Education in Syria and Recommendations for Its Reform), he urged the complete Arabization of the educational system.[77] According to one source, the recommendations contained in these reports were largely adopted

[75] Syria had been granted independence in 1941 when British and Free French forces took over the country from the Vichy authorities. France, however, attempted to keep control of both Syria and Lebanon and insisted on a privileged cultural position in the area. These policies and their results are discussed in Albert H. Hourani, *Syria and Lebanon*, London, 1946, pp. 236-258, 279-307.

[76] Sati el Hussri (al-Husri), "Syria. Post-Mandatory Developments," in *The Year Book of Education, 1949*, London, 1949, pp. 440-441.

[77] Brief accounts of al-Husri's activities in Syria may be found in 'Umar Farukh and Mustafa Khaladi, *al-Tabshir wa al-isti'mar fi al-bilad al-'arabiyyah* (Missionary Activity and Imperialism in the Arab Countries), Beirut, 1953, pp. 82-84; el Hussri, "Syria," pp. 440-447; *Man huwa fi Suriyyah* (Who's Who in Syria), Damascus, 1949, p. 117; Roderic D. Matthews and Matta Akrawi, *Education in Arab Countries of the Near East*, Washington, D.C., 1949, pp. 325-326.

and, while controversial, provided the basis for the postwar educational organization in Syria.[78]

One of the controversies centered around a provision in the Educational Law of 1944 which eliminated the study of foreign languages in primary schools. This clearly bears al-Husri's imprint, and he has noted that the Syrian parliament regarded the passage of this law "as the act of Declaration of Cultural Independence."[79] Strong opposition was also aroused by the essentially secular orientation of al-Husri's program as he once again sought to reform religious institutions and limit the power of religious instructors. When he decided to raise the minimum standard for passing examinations the discontented elements coalesced and in November 1946 students in Damascus demonstrated against his educational reforms with the cry: "There is no God but God and Sati' al-Husri is the enemy of God."[80] As a result, al-Husri resigned and left Damascus for Beirut; but the Syrian government adhered to the reforms.

Continuing his activities in Cairo, where he took up residence in 1947, al-Husri served as adviser to the Cultural Committee of the Arab League, delivered lectures on nationalism and education at Cairo University, and in 1953 was appointed the first director of the Institute of Higher

78 Matthews and Akrawi, *Education*, p. 326.

79 el Hussri, "Syria," p. 441. See also Matthews and Akrawi, *Education*, p. 326; and al-Husri, *Hawliyyat al-thaqafah al-'arabiyyah* (The Yearbook of Arab Culture), I, *1948-1949*, Cairo, 1949, pp. 73-188, for detailed treatment of the law of 1944 as well as statistical information on Syrian education in general immediately after World War II. Cf. Albert Hourani, "Independence and the Imperial Legacy," *Middle East Forum*, XLII, no. 3 (1966), p. 22, where Syria after 1945 is taken as an example of a country in which an overemphasis on the indigenous language and culture can lower the standard of education.

80 This incident is related in an article by Ahmad Amin, "Ma'sah" (A Tragedy), *al-Thaqafah*, no. 415 (December 1946).

Arab Studies. Including students from all the Arab countries, striving to raise the general level of Arab education in all fields, and expounding a philosophy of Arab nationalism and unity, this institution can be regarded, at least in the hopes which he held for it, as the culmination of al-Husri's educational theories in action.[81] He continued to direct it with tremendous energy but growing disenchantment until his retirement from all official duties in 1957, at the age of 77.

But the burning concern for the cause he championed did not end. From his sparse room in Cairo's Pension Viennoise, and later from Beirut and Baghdad, where he died in December 1968, a steady stream of publications flowed from his pen elaborating on the doctrines of Arab nationalism and unity which he had expounded for nearly half a century. It is to an analysis of these doctrines that attention will now be turned.

[81] See al-Husri, *al-Muhadarah al-iftitahiyyah* (The Inaugural Lecture), Cairo, 1954, pp. 21-22, in which he states the general educational goals of the Institute and then adds: "We expect the achievements of this institution to have another result, more important and more noble than all those mentioned above. Namely, the stimulation of the nationalist awakening in the Arab world by spreading matters concerned with the Arab nation and by increasing the hopes for its future." A translation of the charter of the Institute and a list of the original staff members may be found in *Mélanges de L'Institut Dominicain d'Études Orientales du Caire*, I, 1954, Cairo, 1954, pp. 172-175. See also Burj, *al-Husri*, pp. 84-91, for a description of al-Husri's attitude toward the Institute.

PART TWO

The Arab Nationalist Thought of Sati' al-Husri

CHAPTER

3

Defining the Nation

Introduction

As has been seen, the defeat of the Ottoman Empire in World War I resulted in the partition and occupation of its Arab provinces. Foreign mandates were imposed in Palestine, Greater Syria, Iraq, and Transjordan. British forces also remained in Egypt which had been declared a protectorate during the war. This occupation disrupted the Ottoman system under which the Arab provinces had been governed by a central administration, and the resulting political division tended to obscure the vague concept of an Arab state which had emerged during the war. In addition, not only was the temporal authority of the Ottoman Empire destroyed, but the religious ties which had bound the Muslim majority of Arabs to the Ottoman caliph were also severed by Atatürk's abolition of the office of the caliphate in 1924.[1]

Arab responses to this situation took different directions.[2]

1 For Atatürk's policies toward the caliphate, see Berkes, *Development*, pp. 457-460; Lewis, *Emergence*, pp. 256-260.

2 They are examined in, among others, Charles F. Gallagher, "Lan-

Some felt that Arab identity should continue to be expressed in broad Islamic terms and sought the revival of a strictly Arab caliphate. In the decade following the war, a series of general caliphate and Islamic congresses were held in Cairo, Mecca, and Jerusalem, affirming the necessity of the caliphate and the desirability of its restoration in Arab hands.[3] Other Arab intellectuals and political leaders expressed, with varying degrees of emphasis on Islamic or Christian ties, their loyalties to the special heritage of their own particular region. In this manner, the Pharaonism of Egypt, the Phoenicianism of Lebanon and Syria, and a host of other regional doctrines were developed. All of them threatened to solidify the externally imposed divisions by creating loyalty to a specific area at the expense of broader Arab unity. Still other Arab thinkers began to develop more fully the idea that the Arabs constituted a nation and that a new basis of secular loyalty and identification should be constructed around that nation. To substitute the heretofore alien concept of secular nation in place of previously accepted religious solidarity signified an important innova-

---

guage, Culture, and Ideology," in K. H. Silvert (ed.), *Expectant Peoples*, New York, 1967, esp. pp. 212-224; Haim, *Arab Nationalism*, pp. 34-49; Hourani, *Arabic Thought*, pp. 289-298; Kemal H. Karpat (ed.), *Political and Social Thought in the Contemporary Middle East*, New York, 1968, pp. 27-32; Khadduri, *Political Trends*, pp. 176-211; Hazem Zaki Nuseibeh, *The Ideas of Arab Nationalism*, Ithaca, 1956, pp. 148-159; and Labib Zuwiyya-Yamak's superb introduction to his *The Syrian Social Nationalist Party*, Cambridge, Mass., 1966.

[3] The most detailed treatment of the first two congresses is found in Achille Sekaly, "Les deux Congrès Généraux de 1926," *Revue du Monde Musulman*, LXIV, no. 2 (1926). For the congress held at Jerusalem, see H.A.R. Gibb, "The Islamic Congress at Jerusalem in December 1931," in *Survey of International Affairs, 1934*, London, 1935, pp. 99-109.

tion in Arabic thought.[4] Anathema to some, the only possible means of progress to others, secular pan-Arab nationalism found one of its first and most enduring spokesman in Sati' al-Husri.

Al-Husri was at once representative and precursor: in the necessity of reconciling former Ottoman loyalties with post-war Arabism, he was not alone; but in articulating the consequences of this new identity, he was perhaps the first to call for total Arab unity exclusive of Islamic ties.[5] He was a secular pan-Arab nationalist in an area of the world where secularism was not yet accepted, nationalism was little understood, and unity not universally desired.

Sylvia Haim correctly remarks that al-Husri's thought is seldom original.[6] He was not the creator of a political or intellectual system, and his concepts were drawn mainly from nineteenth century European thinkers. His intellectual introduction to Europe had been through the medium of the French language, his first intellectual synthesis had centered around French scientific popularizers, sociologists, and educators, and he himself was largely a man of French culture and outlook. His ideas on nationalism, however, stemmed more from the German romantic nationalists.

4 Haim, *Arab Nationalism*, p. 39; Zuwiyya-Yamak, *Nationalist Party*, p. 13.

5 Mustafa Kamil (1874-1908) established a national movement in Egypt and Lutfi al-Sayyid (1872-1963) provided a secular ideology for this movement. It was, however, a local, Egyptian-oriented nationalism. Lutfi al-Sayyid even described the idea of Arab unity as pure fantasy. See Jemal Mohammed Ahmed, *The Intellectual Origins of Egyptian Nationalism*, London, 1960, pp. 76-112; Hourani, *Arabic Thought*, pp. 170-182; Nadav Safran, *Egypt in Search of Political Community*, Cambridge, Mass., 1961, pp. 85-97. Al-Sayyid's attitude toward Arab unity is cited in Haim, *Arab Nationalism*, p. 48.

6 Haim, *Arab Nationalism*, p. 43.

Whereas his position as an Ottoman had forced him initially to reject the German theorists of linguistic nationalism, he later found in them his principal historical argument when applied directly to the Arab situation.[7] To al-Husri, this represented not so much the espousal of newly understood concepts as it did the intellectual response of a man who had seen the failure of one doctrine, a broad-based Ottomanism in this case, and was able to propose another which was more suited to the changed situation. Because of his solid background in Western nationalist literature, he was able to make the intellectual transition from Ottoman to Arab nationalist quite rapidly. His Arab nationalism represented the utilitarian employment of what he considered the only doctrines applicable to the existing conditions. He quoted favorably from Arndt, Herder, and Hegel, but was particularly impressed by Fichte, regarding the *Addresses to the German Nation* as one of the most important contributions to the ideology of nationalism.[8] This was both because of the content of these speeches in relation to the importance of language, history, unification, and national education, and also because of the action-oriented nature of Fichte's message. Fichte spoke especially to youth as

[7] Al-Husri told the author that of all the European thinkers he had read, he felt that the German theorists and the example of German nationalism were the most instructive for the needs of the Arabs. Interview with Sati' al-Husri, September 28, 1966.

[8] See, for example, al-Husri's "Bayn al-wataniyyah wa al-ummumiyyah" (Between Patriotism and Internationalism), in *Ara' wa ahadith fi al-wataniyyah wa al-qawmiyyah* (Views and Discussions on Patriotism and Nationalism), 4th ed., Beirut, 1961. Hereafter cited *al-Wataniyyah*. This essay was originally delivered as a lecture to the Muthanna Club in Baghdad in 1937. See also al-Husri, *Ma hiya al-qawmiyyah?* (What Is Nationalism?), 2nd ed., Beirut, 1963, pp. 57-64; and *Nushu' al-fikrah al-qawmiyyah*, pp. 33-37.

al-Husri tried to do, both men feeling that the inspiration of this segment of society could lead to the implementation of their ideals. In what he attempted to achieve, in what he felt was his mission, al-Husri was not unlike the Fichte of the *Addresses to the German Nation.*

Al-Husri found a similar deep admiration for Pestalozzi as a man whose thought and actions complemented each other perfectly. In his private libraries from Istanbul to Baghdad, a bust of the Swiss educator was on prominent display and he was once moved to write: "We, too, acclaim Pestalozzi. We venerate that spirit which is embodied in his honorable name: the spirit of the true teacher, the spirit of sacrifice, the spirit of striving toward the highest ideal, the spirit of courage and perseverance, the spirit of faith in education."[9]

His work also contains sentiments which resemble those of Ziya Gökalp, whose Turkish nationalism al-Husri had previously opposed. Yet there was a substantial difference between the basic experiences of these two nationalist ideologues, a difference which was reflected in their appreciation of the synthesis between culture and civilization and their attitude toward the role of Islam in society. Gökalp's lack of firsthand knowledge of Europe and his limited understanding of its culture prompted him to ignore the link between Western spiritual culture and its material achievements. He believed that the influence of Western civilization in Turkey could be restricted to the natural sciences and technical subjects without penetrating the spheres which he felt belonged to national culture.[10] The

[9] Al-Husri, "Pestalozzi," *Majallah al-tarbiyah wa al-ta'lim,* I, no. 3 (1928), p. 168.

[10] See Heyd, *Foundations,* p. 81.

case was different with al-Husri. A cosmopolitan who rejected cosmopolitanism, al-Husri was no less involved in his society than Gökalp was in his. But there was a deeper understanding on al-Husri's part of the forces that had shaped Western civilization and a more direct attempt to impose those forces on the Arabs. Sylvia Haim has made the very appropriate observation that it is Fichte rather than the Quran which inspires al-Husri.[11]

Like his German models, al-Husri's approach to nationalism was on a cultural, romantic plane. His ideology of Arab nationalism was not formulated in an attempt to obtain political liberties, but rather for the purpose of inspiring the sentiments required to produce national unity. Thus, as was the case in the genesis of German nationalism, al-Husri first defined the nation as a cultural rather than a political entity.[12] In this respect, the words of Hans Kohn about the patriotic German poet Arndt are equally applicable to al-Husri in his time and place: "He had no clear concept of German political unity, nor did he foresee the road to its realization, but he emphasized the need of new and stronger ties for the German Reich and promised to devote all his strength to awakening the demand for it and to keeping the thought of it alive."[13] A similar romanticism was

[11] Haim, "Islam and the Theory of Arab Nationalism," p. 294. See also Karpat, *Political and Social Thought*, pp. 55-56, for a brief comparison between the ideas of al-Husri and Gökalp.

[12] Helpful in understanding this type of nationalism are two articles by Hans Kohn, "The Eve of German Nationalism (1789-1812)," *Journal of the History of Ideas*, XII, no. 2 (1951), pp. 256-284; and "Romanticism and the Rise of German Nationalism," *The Review of Politics*, XII, no. 4 (1950), pp. 443-472. See also the excellent contribution by Otto Pflanze, "Nationalism in Europe, 1848-1871," *The Review of Politics*, XXVIII, no. 2 (1966), pp. 129-143.

[13] Hans Kohn, "Arndt and the Character of German Nationalism," *The American Historical Review*, LIV, no. 4 (1949), p. 788.

characteristic of the other leading Arab nationalist writers of the inter-war period with whom al-Husri's works have been compared.[14] What Otto Pflanze has called "the diversionary influence of nationalism" whereby nationalist sentiments tend to channel appeals away from certain fundamental issues of social justice and political freedom was typical of Arab nationalism at this time and, as will be shown, was particularly evident in al-Husri's works.[15]

In a further resemblance to his German models, al-Husri viewed the nation as a spiritual, living being and placed great emphasis on the naturalness of national existence. But where Arndt, for example, wrote that in language and descent Germany excelled over all other nations and thus had a creative superiority, al-Husri restricted his call to a more limited context and urged pride in Arab civilization without expressing a corresponding sense of comparative racial superiority.[16] He further differed from the German romantic nationalists in that he did not call upon the Arabs

14 In conjunction with al-Husri's contributions, Constantine Zurayq's *al-Wa'y al-qawmi* (National Consciousness [1938]), 'Abd Allah al-'Alayili's *Dustur al-'arab al-qawmi* (The National Constitution of the Arabs [1938]), and 'Ali Nasir al-Din's *Qadiyyat al-'arab* (The Arab Case [1946]), are generally recognized as the outstanding initial attempts to introduce the basic concepts of nationalism and unity to the Arabs. For a comparison of their views see Naji 'Allush, "al-Harakah al-'arabiyyah ba'd al-harb al-'alamiyyah al-ula" (The Arab Movement after the First World War), *Dirasat 'arabiyyah*, II, no. 2 (1965), pp. 65-69; Nuseibeh, *Ideas*, pp. 68-70, 77-78, 84-85; Shimon Shamir, "The Question of a 'National Philosophy' in Contemporary Arab Thought," *Asian and African Studies*, I (1965), p. 4. Despite similar basic objectives, these authors probably derived their inspiration from different sources—Hourani suggests in *Arabic Thought*, p. 312, that al-Husri is the only Arab nationalist who seems to have read Fichte.

15 Pflanze, "Nationalism," pp. 131-132.

16 Cf. Kohn, "Arndt," p. 791.

to undertake a worldwide civilizing mission nor did he have faith in a higher order which directed the affairs of mankind toward progress.[17] One of his principal innovations in the Arab world was his very attempt to diminish the influence of religion in general through the advocacy of secular bonds of loyalty to the Arab nation.

Al-Husri's intellectual efforts to forge a secular pan-Arab national identity rest largely on his special interpretation of history, and he frequently used historical examples as propaganda devices. For all his wide-ranging abilities and his truly remarkable mind, al-Husri was not a detached intellectual and he must be viewed within the context of his times and analyzed by what he attempted to do. As the protagonist of a cause, he presented only that which was propitious to his cause. He had an objective to which he rigidly adhered, and if he sometimes distorted or simplified history, it was because his objective was best served by such a presentation. His was a response to a particular set of personal and historical circumstances, the collapse of the old order and his own position within that order, and the attempt to formulate a new one on the basis of secular nationalism.

Al-Husri possessed a spare but forceful literary style, one which was quite direct in its approach to the issues which he raised, but which was also capable of occasional imagery. He most often presented his arguments in self-contained essays which employed the following organization: he stated a premise which he favored, buttressed it with the "historical and scientific facts," and then said that these facts proved the irrefutable validity of the initial

[17] Al-Husri termed Fichte's concepts on this matter "Sufi-like." See al-Husri, *Nushu' al-fikrah al-qawmiyyah*, p. 36.

premise which was forcefully repeated as a conclusion.[18] Another device which al-Husri often used was to recognize and predict the doubts his audience might have concerning a statement which he had just made, and then to demolish those rhetorical doubts with even more facts. It was an effective and convincing method when combined with his wide reading and his ability to grasp and manipulate what he had read.

Partially because of this readable and convincing style, but more basically because of the continuing relevance of the questions he treated, al-Husri's work remains immensely popular.[19] This is true even at a time in the history of Arab nationalism when doctrinal parties have taken over the political and intellectual management of the nationalist movement. Al-Husri's constant repetition of his analysis of the constituents of Arab nationhood indicates that to him, and apparently to a large number of the reading public who buy his books, the relevance of his basic premises did not diminish. The presence of new editions of his works, many of which contain essays written nearly four decades ago, underline the unresolved issues which have continued to lie at the heart of the Arab search for national identity since the end of the First World War.

In this search, al-Husri has played a prominent intellectual role. The clarity with which he articulated his doctrines, the unceasing effort which he devoted to spread them, and the emotional intensity with which they are projected make him one of the most important ideologues of

[18] See, for example, al-Husri, *al-Qawmiyyah al-'arabiyyah*, pp. 52-57; and *Nushu' al-fikrah al-qawmiyyah*, p. 61.

[19] This popularity was attested in a conversation with the Director of Dar al-'Ilm, the publishing firm which now prints most of al-Husri's works.

Arab nationalism.[20] Part scientific pedagogue and part passionate ideologue, he proposed a coherent and uncompromising doctrine of Arab nationalism intended to direct the loyalties of all Arabs toward a unified national state.

The Concept of Nation: General Definitions

TERMINOLOGY

Before exploring in depth al-Husri's main themes, a preliminary discussion of his basic terminology will be undertaken. Shortly after he joined the Arabs, al-Husri articulated the general definitions and principles of nationalism to which he committed himself for the rest of his career.[21]

Essential to his thought is his clarification of the terms patriotism and nationalism, concepts which to him represent the two single most important ties binding individuals to each other. Patriotism (*al-wataniyyah*) is love of the fatherland (*al-watan*) and a feeling of inward commitment (*irtibat batini*) toward it; nationalism (*al-qawmiyyah*) is love of the nation (*al-ummah*) and a similar feeling of inward commitment. The nation is defined as a group of human

20 Haim, *Arab Nationalism*, p. 43. Cf. Hourani, *Arabic Thought*, pp. 311, 343; Kenny, "al-Husri's Views," p. 231.

21 Insofar as possible, the following discussion will take into account the chronological presentation of al-Husri's thought. Those items, which were written as separate essays and lectures, will be noted with their dates and titles along with the collection in which they have been reprinted. The earliest al-Husri statement of nationalism available to us is a lecture delivered at Dar al-Mu'allimin in Baghdad in 1923 entitled "al-Wataniyyah wa al-qawmiyyah" (Patriotism and Nationalism). It appears in *Abhath mukhtarah fi al-qawmiyyah al-'arabiyyah* (Selected Studies on Arab Nationalism), Cairo, 1964, pp. 28-36; and in *al-Wataniyyah*, pp. 9-22. Our references will be to *Abhath mukhtarah*. All future references will be to al-Husri's works unless otherwise noted.

beings bound by mutually recognized ties of language and history, and the fatherland as the territory inhabited by this special group of people.[22] Traditionally used to denote the entire political and religious community of Islam, the word *al-ummah* implies to al-Husri a secular rather than a religious identification. It is the Arab and not the Islamic *ummah* with which he is concerned.[23] A close interrelationship exists between patriotism and nationalism since love of the fatherland naturally entails a love for the people inhabiting it, and, similarly, love of the nation implies a love of the land on which that nation lies.[24]

When *al-watan* and *al-wataniyyah* are applied in the broadest sense by al-Husri, they appear to be almost interchangeable with *al-ummah* and *al-qawmiyyah*. From the general tone of his works, however, it is evident that *al-ummah* is a higher concept than *al-watan* and that loyalty to the nation is a correspondingly nobler sentiment. Al-Husri clarifies this to some extent by distinguishing between two general types of *watan*: *al-watan al-khass* (the particular fatherland), which is limited by the borders of the state; and *al-watan al-'amm* (the general fatherland) which includes all the territory in which the people of the *ummah* live, regardless of the political separations which may exist within that territory. Al-Husri's preference for this latter type of *watan* is indicated by his qualification of it with the adjectives *al-mithali* (ideal), *al-manshud* (desired), and *al-qawmi* (national). Nationalists, he declares,

22 "Al-Wataniyyah wa al-qawmiyyah," in *Abhath mukhtarah*, p. 28. See also the discussion of al-Husri's nationalist vocabulary in Kenny, "al-Husri's Views," pp. 232-234.

23 Cf. Haim, "Islam and the Theory of Arab Nationalism," pp. 287-288.

24 "Al-Wataniyyah wa al-qawmiyyah," in *Abhath mukhtarah*, pp. 28, 32.

are those who direct their hearts toward the ideal fatherland and who seek to unite the people of one nation under a single banner.[25] A further refinement is introduced by the notion of the state (*al-dawlah*) which is strictly a political entity, a sovereign independent group of people living on a common land within fixed borders.[26] Al-Husri contends that a failure to differentiate properly between state and nation has led to confusion among scholars attempting to deal with these two concepts. As an example, he points to the Encyclopedists for whom the central qualification of both state and nation was a group of people living under one government.[27] This is unacceptable to al-Husri who declares that in such a definition the people of Berlin, Bonn, and Frankfort would have been regarded as being from different nations because they belonged to different states. Similarly, the peoples of Vienna, Budapest, Prague, and Zaghreb would have been considered as being from one nation because they were under one state, the Hapsburg Empire. Al-Husri believes that French scholars were slow in differentiating these important concepts because France achieved her national-statehood at such an early date. They used the word *nationalité* to express both an individual's legal citizenship in a state and his social membership in a nation.[28] The Germans, on the other hand, because of the divided nature of their nation until 1870, clearly distinguished between the two concepts by using the word *Nationalität* to express legal citizenship and the separate

25 *Al-Qawmiyyah al-'arabiyyah,* pp. 24-25.

26 "Al-Wataniyyah wa al-qawmiyyah," in *Abhath mukhtarah,* p. 28.

27 *Ma hiya al-qawmiyyah?,* pp. 33-34.

28 *Ibid.,* pp. 35-38; and a lecture delivered in Cairo in 1950, "al-Qawmiyyah al-'arabiyyah" (Arab Nationalism), in *al-Qawmiyyah al-'arabiyyah,* p. 41. See above, pp. 36-37, for al-Husri's discussion of French and German national development in *Vatan İçin.*

term *Volkstum* to denote social membership in a nation.[29] Al-Husri finds the German example applicable to the Arabs and explains that the legal concept is included in the terms *al-jinsiyyah, al-tabi'iyyah,* and *al-ra'awiyyah,* while the social concept is expressed by *al-qawmiyyah. Al-qawmiyyah* thus refers to membership in a nation as well as to the sentiment of nationalism.[30]

The optimum confluence of these concepts exists when a nation consists of a single state ruling territory which is regarded as a fatherland by all the inhabitants of the nation. In such an instance, nationalism and patriotism completely correspond. A less fortunate situation occurs when the nation is divided into a number of independent states, each evoking its own patriotism. In this case nationalism is incompatible with the local patriotisms; it strives to reach beyond them, to work for the unification of the scattered states into a single national state and to create a feeling of patriotism which transcends the limited state boundaries.[31] This situation is exemplified by Germany before its unification. Other disruptions occur when nations possess neither independence nor a state, such as Bulgaria in the middle of the nineteenth century or Poland after its partitions.[32] But these circumstances do not negate the presence of a nation. Al-Husri makes it very clear that a nation's existence is not

29 *Ma hiya al-qawmiyyah?,* p. 35; "al-Qawmiyyah al-'arabiyyah," in *al-Qawmiyyah al-'arabiyyah,* p. 42.

30 *Al-Qawmiyyah al-'arabiyyah,* p. 43. Cf. Kenny, "al-Husri's Views," p. 234. A critique of al-Husri's definitions in which it is argued, incorrectly, that he provides the form of nationalism with an existence independent of the substance of the nation may be found in Sami Khuri, *Radd 'ala Sati' al-Husri* (A Reply to Sati' al-Husri), Beirut, n.d. [1956], pp. 22-23.

31 "Al-Wataniyyah wa al-qawmiyyah," in *Abhath mukhtarah,* p. 29; *al-Qawmiyyah al-'arabiyyah,* p. 24.

32 *Al-Qawmiyyah al-'arabiyyah,* p. 30.

dependent on the founding of a state. Rather, the nation is a continually existing entity. The awakening of nationalism will bring the recognition of this entity and the desire to see it constitute a true national state.[33]

"Arabism" (*al-'urubah*) is another word frequently employed by al-Husri. It is less a definable term than an emotive symbol signifying the existence of Arabness, the embodiment of Arab nationalism and a belief in Arab unity. A similar connotation is given to the word "culture" (*al-thaqafah*) which is regarded as an amalgam of Arab civilization, its language and its history, and the present shared outlook which should exist because of them. Before all these concepts can provide the impetus for national unification, they have to be recognized, the emotions embodied in them released, and unequivocal identification with the Arab nation must be asserted. In order to show that the Arabs do indeed constitute a nation composed of elements similar to those of other nations, al-Husri presents his national definitions within a carefully demarcated historical context.

THE EVIDENCE OF HISTORY

Al-Husri's approach to history is not stated in terms of the debate over political liberties and the rights of individuals. He posits the nation instead, and the form of government is irrelevant. To be free does not mean the possession of constitutionalism or democracy, but of national unity. In his interpretation, the French Revolution has been overstudied since it simply led to a change in the system of governments, and left the nature of states unaffected. It therefore possesses none of the significance of the national

[33] *Ma hiya al-qawmiyyah?*, pp. 34, 38.

revolts which followed it.[34] The notion of the rights of the people is historically meaningful to al-Husri primarily in the sense that through it people began to discover the unique character of the nation to which they belonged in contradistinction to the political state of which they were citizens. It was this recognition which gave birth to the principle of nationalities and the spread of nationalism which then "began to rule over the course of history," awakening previously dormant nations from their sleep, making them aware of their special existence, and driving them to strengthen that existence through the creation of a national state in which the boundaries of the nation and the political state would be identical.[35] The remarkable changes that took place in the map of Europe in the late nineteenth and early twentieth centuries, from the unification of Italy and Germany to the dissolution of Austria-Hungary and the Ottoman Empire, can be explained only in terms of the spread of nationalism in the souls of the people.[36]

Because of the overwhelming significance he attributes to the force of nationalism in modern history, al-Husri has analyzed in countless passages the components of the nation and the sentiments of nationalism and patriotism. These

[34] *Ibid.*, pp. 7-10; *al-Muhadarah al-iftitahiyyah*, pp. 10-13; *Nushu' al-fikrah al-qawmiyyah*, pp. 13-14. He does admit that the Napoleonic Empire created new states and destroyed old ones, but he considers this a short-lived phenomenon ending with the restoration of the old order at Vienna. Al-Husri's concept of personal freedom will be discussed in more detail below, pp. 165-170.

[35] " 'Awamil al-qawmiyyah" (The Factors of Nationalism), in *Abhath mukhtarah*, p. 38. This essay was originally delivered as a lecture in Baghdad in 1928.

[36] *Nushu' al-fikrah al-qawmiyyah*, pp. 3-14. See also *Ma hiya al-qawmiyyah?*, p. 28; "al-Wataniyyah wa al-qawmiyyah," in *Abhath mukhtarah*, pp. 31-32.

concepts themselves were new in the Arab world, and al-Husri considered it his duty to repeat them and make them familiar. One of his more frequent methods is through a series of rhetorical questions: "What is a nation? What are the basic characteristics which distinguish nations from each other? What are the factors which make some groups of people feel that they are one nation and therefore desire to strengthen their existence by creating a special state?"[37]

These are enduring questions to al-Husri and, in combination with his replies given below, should be viewed as the foundations of his theoretical exposition of nationalism. From the important Baghdad lecture of 1923, "al-Wataniyyah wa al-qawmiyyah," to a more recent essay in *al-'Urubah awwalan* both questions and answers remained constant.[38] The historical context remained constant also in the general sense that the Arab nation achieved neither unity nor total recognition from all its inhabitants. Al-Husri could therefore continually address himself to the same basic questions, regarding them as pertinent to the Arab situation. And just as he acknowledged that scholars have given different answers to these questions in accordance with the interests and positions of their own nations, so must any study of al-Husri recognize that his own selection of evidence and interpretation of history were conditioned

[37] *Ma hiya al-qawmiyyah?*, p. 31.

[38] Haim contends that no serious attempt was made to define Arab nationalism and the components of the Arab nation until the 1930s, *Arab Nationalism*, p. 35. But al-Husri's concern with these issues originates from the decade preceding Haim's starting point. It is true that he published nothing on nationalism in book form at this date, but he reached a wide audience in Iraq because of his influence on the educational system. It is likely that his frequent contributions to newspapers and journals made his views well known to the intellectual community outside Iraq also.

by the nature of the Arab situation and his own relation to it.

Al-Husri answered the above questions with an explicit declaration that language and history are the two most important components of nationhood. Passage after passage in various books, articles, and speeches reaffirm his continuing belief in the paramountcy of these two elements as the exclusively fundamental factors in distinguishing nations from each other and in inspiring the national awareness leading to unity. The following statement is typical:

> The foundations for creating the nation and building nationalism are unity of language and history. This is because unity in these two spheres leads to unity of feelings and inclinations, unity of sufferings and hopes, and unity of culture, thus making the people feel that they are the sons of one nation, distinguished from other nations.[39]

Of these two factors, language is the most crucial. In a lecture of 1928 entitled, " 'Awamil al-qawmiyyah" (The Factors of Nationalism), he elaborated on the role of language in the following manner:

> Language is the most important spiritual tie which binds mankind. First, it is the means of mutual understanding among individuals. In addition, it is the instrument of thought. . . . Finally, language is the means of transmission for ideas and acquired knowledge from fathers to sons, from ancestors to descendants. The language with which man grows up molds his thought in a special manner just as it deeply influences his sentiments. . . . Therefore, it is found that unity of language establishes a kind of unity of thought and feeling which binds individuals with a long and interconnected series of sentimental and intellectual ties. We can say that language is

[39] *Abhath mukhtarah*, p. 249. Cf. *al-'Urubah bayn du'atiha wa mu'aridiha* (Arabism between Its Proponents and Antagonists), 4th ed., Beirut, 1961, p. 96.

> the strongest of the ties which bind individuals to groups. Since languages differ between races, it is natural that we find groups of individuals who share the same language drawing nearer to each other than to other groups. Thus, we can say that nations are distinguished from each other first by their language, and that the life of nations is based before everything else on their language.[40]

To al-Husri, then, "language is the life and spirit of the nation; it is like the heart and spine of nationalism, the most important of its components and characteristics."[41] As the very life of a nation, language is so indispensable that its loss means the loss of the nation's existence as well. But the loss of political independence does not mean the loss of existence if the nation's language is preserved, for "a subjugated nation which preserves its language is like a prisoner whose hand grasps the key to his prison."[42] In the case of Poland, for example, al-Husri contends that even though the state disappeared after the final partition, the nation remained, preserved in language and history, and was eventually reunited as a national state.[43]

Al-Husri goes to some lengths to justify fully this

40 " 'Awamil al-qawmiyyah" in *Abhath mukhtarah*, pp. 42-43; see also *Nushu' al-fikrah al-qawmiyyah*, pp. 20-21, for a nearly identical statement. For the articulation of similar sentiments by Fichte and Herder, both of whom al-Husri admired, see Johann Gottlieb Fichte, *Addresses to the German Nation*, trans. by R. F. Jones and G. H. Turnbull, Chicago, 1922, pp. 69-71; and Robert Rheinhold Ergang, *Herder and the Foundations of German Nationalism*, New York, 1931, pp. 148-150.

41 " 'Awamil al-qawmiyyah," in *Abhath mukhtarah*, p. 44; "Bayn al-madi wa al-mustaqbil" (Between the Past and the Future), in *al-Wataniyyah*, pp. 109-110. This essay originally appeared in the journal *al-Risalah*, v, no. 233 (1937).

42 " 'Awamil al-qawmiyyah," in *Abhath mukhtarah*, pp. 43-44.

43 "Al-Qawmiyyah al-'arabiyyah," in *al-Qawmiyyah al-'arabiyyah*, pp. 36-37.

interpretation of the force and influence of language. He explains the situation of Belgium and Switzerland by denying that they constitute true nations. They are both states, but the absence of a national language prevents them from being considered nations. Geography in the case of Switzerland, and the play of the balance of power in the case of Belgium have prevented the absorption of the diverse language groups within these two states by the neighboring national states.[44] The interpretation of history in these terms further demands from al-Husri an explanation of how the United States separated from England during the American Revolution. In a rather tortuous and unconvincing argument, he points out that this took place before the age of nationalism, that geography, which he usually denies as a motive factor, played a significant role, and that language differences, which he grossly overstates, caused by the influx of European immigrants, were not yet assimilated into English.[45] Consistency for his theory is maintained further by al-Husri's explanation for the existence of an independent German-speaking Austria. He gives full recognition to the German interests of the Hapsburgs and the conflicts over the Austrian or Prussian leadership of the German unification movement. He then concludes that conditions within the Austro-Hungarian Empire, such as its sectarian Catholic policies and the comparatively small number of Germans among its subjects, prevented it from assuming the German leadership. Nevertheless, argues al-Husri, the Germans in Austria desired union with their German-speak-

[44] *Ma hiya al-qawmiyyah?*, pp. 92-106; "Bayn Misr wa al-'urubah" (Between Egypt and Arabism), in *al-Wataniyyah*, pp. 126-129. This essay originally appeared in the journal *al-Risalah*, VI, no. 285 (1938).

[45] *Ma hiya al-qawmiyyah?*, pp. 73-77; *al-'Urubah bayn du'atiha wa mu'aridiha*, pp. 93-94. Cf. Kenny, "al-Husri's Views," p. 239.

ing brethren and after each of the two world wars it was only Allied action which prevented this natural union.[46]

As language gives the nation life and spirit, so history provides it with feelings and memories:

> Unity of history gives rise to shared feelings and outlooks. It leads to common memories of bygone exploits and past misfortunes, and to a mutual faith in the awakening and to mutually shared hopes for the future. . . . Every nation feels its self-consciousness and creates its personality by means of its special history.[47]

The importance of history is evidenced by the fact that whenever ruling nations conquer another nation, they attempt to suppress the voice of that nation's history through the substitution of their own version of history.[48] A nation which forgets its history loses its feelings and self-consciousness, although these can be revived if the language remains.

Al-Husri's brand of history, in this regard, is given a special definition: "When I say history, I do not mean that history recorded in books and buried between the pages of manuscripts—I mean that history which lives in the people, which is universally known in the minds and which possesses traditions."[49] This conveys a mystical understanding of the nation as a living force and is underlined in another essay in which al-Husri writes: "The nation is a living

[46] *Ma hiya al-qawmiyyah?*, pp. 85-91. It is still unclear how al-Husri explains the resolution of the *Grossdeutsch-Kleindeutsch* conflict in favor of the latter.

[47] "'Awamil al-qawmiyyah," in *Abhath mukhtarah*, p. 44; and *Nushu' al-fikrah al-qawmiyyah*, p. 21.

[48] "'Awamil al-qawmiyyah," in *Abhath mukhtarah*, p. 44; "Bayn al-madi wa al-mustaqbil," in *al-Wataniyyah*, pp. 109-110; "al-'Ilm li al-'ilm am al-'ilm li al-watan?" (Knowledge for the Sake of Knowledge or the Sake of the Fatherland?), in *al-Wataniyyah*, pp. 148-149. This essay originally appeared in the journal *al-Risalah*, v, no. 206 (1937).

[49] "'Awamil al-qawmiyyah," in *Abhath mukhtarah*, p. 44.

being, with life and feeling, life through its language and feeling through its history."[50] Adding a further dimension to this concept, al-Husri supports Mazzini's notion of a natural grouping of elements which produce the living nation.[51] From this comes al-Husri's ultimate refinement of the nation and its components as dynamic and organic forces: "The nation is one of the naturally living things, and to life there is strength and to nature there are regulations."[52] Therefore, national unity is both natural and inevitable. As we shall see shortly, the course of history has shown to al-Husri the fulfillment of these regulations.

Synonymous as the natural and the national are in al-Husri's definition, he asserts that the nationalism which sustains nations operates on a spiritual level distinct from the mechanical actions within the organisms of nature. This romantic emphasis on spiritual forces pervades all of al-Husri's work.[53] Phrases such as *ruh al-'urubah* (the spirit of Arabism) and *rawabit ma'nawiyyah* (spiritual ties) appear repeatedly. He draws not only on the German nationalists for this belief in the predominant significance of spiritual as opposed to material ties, but also on Ibn Khaldun whom he has studied more carefully than he has any other medieval Arab author.[54] To al-Husri, the theory of

50 *Al-Qawmiyyah al-'arabiyyah*, p. 69.

51 *Ma hiya al-qawmiyyah?*, pp. 41-42.

52 "Al-Iman al-qawmi" (The National Faith), an undated [1935?] lecture delivered to the Muthanna Club in Baghdad, in *Abhath mukhtarah*, p. 113.

53 It continues to dominate the works of a younger generation of Arab nationalists as well. See Shamir, "National Philosophy," pp. 15-16.

54 See his detailed work, *Dirasat 'an muqaddimah Ibn Khaldun* (Studies on the Muqaddimah of Ibn Khaldun), first published in two volumes in Beirut, 1943-1944, and reprinted in Cairo in 1961. Future references will be to the Cairo edition. After the birth of his son, al-Husri often identified his works by using the name Abu Khaldun.

'asabiyyah (solidarity) propounded by Ibn Khaldun in the *Muqaddimah* includes more than a communal feeling based only on blood relationships; it is extended to include *le lien social* and *esprit de corps*.[55] It is therefore the spiritual rather than the material nature of cohesive social forces which al-Husri stresses. According to al-Husri, when Ibn Khaldun speaks of kinship and friendship, he says all that springs from the blood relationship of the former can also develop from the natural social solidarity of the latter.[56]

In this manner, the relationship which provides people with a feeling of membership in one nation is a spiritual relationship arising from various social ties which are, in al-Husri's view, a sharing of language and history. Al-Husri declares that because people do not see all of their country nor meet all of its inhabitants, they are bound by spiritual rather than perceptible, material ties to the total national entity.[57] Patriotic and nationalistic feelings are not connected to material benefits, but are above them and resemble maternal love. What al-Husri emphasizes in this sense is that such spiritual sentiments can motivate people to self-sacrifice in a way that material drives never can. This is the role he believes nationalism has performed in the past in Europe and will continue to perform in the non-European

[55] *Dirasat 'an muqaddimah*, pp. 338-339, 351. Al-Husri often has recourse to the Latin alphabet when explaining Western concepts. For more detailed discussions of *'asabiyyah*, see the translator's introduction in Ibn Khaldun, *The Muqaddimah*, trans. by Franz Rosenthal, 3 vols., New York, 1958, vol. I, pp. lxxviii-lxxxiii; and Muhsin Mahdi, *Ibn Khaldun's Philosophy of History*, London, 1957, pp. 196-199.

[56] *Ma hiya al-qawmiyyah?*, p. 44. Cf. *The Muqaddimah*, p. lxxix.

[57] "Al-Wataniyyah wa al-qawmiyyah," in *Abhath mukhtarah*, pp. 32-34. For a somewhat opposing viewpoint in which community of interest is included as a basic component of Arab nationalism, see Nuseibeh, *Ideas*, pp. 84-88.

areas of the world; it awakens sentiments which inspire people to national revolt, unification, and revival: "We must remember that the nationalist idea enjoys a self-motivating power; it is a driving impulse to action and to struggle. When it enters the mind and dominates the soul, it is one of the motive ideas, one of the *idées forces* which awaken the people and inspire them to sacrifice when necessary."[58] The driving elements in these actions have been and continue to be language and history: "When the language became the heart and spirit of the nation, then the people who spoke one language possessed one heart and a common spirit and therefore formed one nation. It then became necessary that they create one state."[59] The very concept of unity (*al-wahdah*) is also imparted a romantic spiritual and motive power by al-Husri. He writes: "Unity in my view is much more exalted than being just a word; it indicates a lofty idea. It is also an efficacious idea and can provide a powerful impetus for making people determined."[60]

With this emphasis on the motive power and spiritual nature of linguistic and historical bonds, al-Husri is led to a refutation of other ties as factors in determining the existence of nations and producing recognition and action on the part of individuals. Some, he explains, argue that unity of origins is an essential element in national composition. Adherents of this view say that the individuals of one nation are descendants of a common ancestor. This doctrine elicits the following comment from al-Husri: "All scientific studies based on the facts of history, the discoveries of anthropology and ethnography leave no doubt that there

[58] *Nushu' al-fikrah al-qawmiyyah,* pp. 238-239.
[59] *Ma hiya al-qawmiyyah?,* p. 55.
[60] *Al-'Urubah bayn du'atiha wa mu'aridiha,* p. 63.

is not found on the face of the earth any nation descended from one origin or possessing pure blood."[61] But the fact of different origins does not negate the existence of a nation. Even France, which al-Husri regards as the first European nation to achieve national unity, was created from an admixture of races which permits recognition of different racial characteristics among its modern inhabitants. In this respect France, like other nations, resembles a great river; it is composed of different sources which have joined it at various intervals to create the recognizable whole. Hence, a Frenchman does not ask if the blood of Charlemagne, Racine, or Voltaire flows in his veins. He simply considers all of them a part of his proud heritage.[62]

Al-Husri also regards as erroneous the conception of the nation proposed by Fustel de Coulanges and later popularized by Ernest Renan in his famous lecture of 1882, "Qu'est ce qu'une nation?"[63] According to this view, "will" is the most important factor in forming nations; a nation is any group of people who will to live together. Feeling that such a concept might serve as a basis of loyalty to the Otto-

61 "'Awamil al-qawmiyyah," in *Abhath mukhtarah*, p. 39; *Nushu' al-fikrah al-qawmiyyah*, p. 19. Cf. Kenny, "al-Husri's Views," p. 236; Nuseibeh, *Ideas*, p. 89. Al-Husri also vehemently criticized the racial theories of Gustave Le Bon for what he termed their pseudo-scientific nature and their denial of the capability of education to promote fundamental transformations among non-Western peoples. See his "Tayyarat al-tarbiyah wa al-ta'lim" (Currents of Pedagogy and Education), *Majallah al-tarbiyah wa al-ta'lim*, I, no. 1 (1928), pp. 43-55. Al-Husri does admit, however, that at times the feeling of a common origin can be a significant unifying factor, even if it is based on incorrect information.

62 "'Awamil al-qawmiyyah," in *Abhath mukhtarah*, pp. 40-41.

63 Ernest Renan (1823-1892) was best known in his century for his confrontation with the problem of science and religion. His lecture on the factors which constitute a nation may be found in his *Discours et conférences*, Paris, n.d. [1887], pp. 276-310.

man Empire, al-Husri was initially attracted to it and defended Renan for a time.[64] But the more he studied history, the more he became convinced that Renan's theory was false, that it resembled the speech of a brilliant lawyer defending a case rather than the truly detached scientific theory of a scholar. He reasons that Renan and his supporters were actually defending the French attempt to secure German-speaking Alsace by countering the German theory of language.[65]

Further expressing his dissatisfaction with this viewpoint, al-Husri argues that Renan, by basing his theory on will alone, has stopped short of the basic inquiry of why some people feel distinct from others and wish to live apart from them in a homogeneous national state of their own. Will, in al-Husri's view, is the result of a shared language and history, the result of national ties rather than an independent formative force in itself.[66] To argue that the will of the masses as expressed in voting is determinative is to support a practice which fluctuates by habit and can be manipulated by propaganda; it is to support a practice which splits the nation from its natural groupings and causes it to resemble artifical parties.[67] This is a further indication of al-Husri's concern for national unity at the possible expense of individual political freedom.

He demonstrates the validity of his own case with his

[64] *Nushu' al-fikrah al-qawmiyyah*, p. 58. Al-Husri continues to favor an approach to historical selectivity reminiscent of Renan. See below, pp. 144-148.

[65] *Ibid.*, pp. 56-57. See also Kenny's discussion in "al-Husri's Views," p. 236.

[66] *Nushu' al-fikrah al-qawmiyyah*, p. 59; *Ma hiya al-qawmiyyah?*, pp. 134-135; "al-Qawmiyyah al-'arabiyyah," in *al-Qawmiyyah al-'arabiyyah*, p. 68.

[67] " 'Awamil al-qawmiyyah," in *Abhath mukhtarah*, p. 52.

favorite debating technique of drawing "irrefutable" examples from history. In this instance, he points out that during the American Civil War the will of the South for separation was quite strong. Yet this will did not continue after the Northern victory because there was no basis in nationality for a separate Southern nation.[68] On the other hand, the series of revolts by Hungary against the Hapsburg Empire in the nineteenth century, even though they initially ended in defeat, continued until the Hungarian nation finally achieved political existence. This will on the part of the Hungarians was sustained because they constituted a nation, different in shared language and history from those of the state which ruled them.[69]

Nor does al-Husri agree with those who argue that economic interests provide a sufficient basis for national unity. While he acknowledges the important role played by such interests in directing the lives of individuals and in influencing the course of history, he nevertheless states that this does not warrant the belief that they form the basis for building unity or "the cornerstone of the lofty edifice of nationalism."[70] This is because economic interests can function as divisive as well as unifying elements.

In addition, it is explained that national unity has been successfully achieved in many countries despite the existence of economic diversity. As examples, al-Husri points to the reconciliation of industrial, commercial, and agricultural interests in the United States; the incorporation of areas of varied interests like Hamburg and Bavaria into a unified Germany, and of Sicily and the northern lakes coun-

68 *Ibid.*, p. 53; *Nushu' al-fikrah al-qawmiyyah*, pp. 61-62.

69 *Nushu' al-fikrah al-qawmiyyah*, pp. 61-62.

70 *Ma hiya al-qawmiyyah?*, p. 161; *al-Qawmiyyah al-'arabiyyah*, p. 78.

try into one Italy.[71] Obviously, al-Husri tends to gloss over the difficulties, historical and contemporary, which have made these mergers sometimes incomplete. It is necessary for him to do this, however, in order to conclude his argument with a declaration that economic and material benefits are not everything in life, that patriotic and national feelings are not tied to such benefits, and that the examples given indicate the necessity of sacrificing a small part of a region for the benefit of the whole.[72]

Quite naturally, al-Husri finds the Marxist interpretation of history unacceptable. Addressing himself to Stalin's work, al-Husri claims that to accept the theory that a common economic life is one of the basic pre-conditions for the creation of a nation is to force one to admit that the Italians did not constitute a nation before completing their unification or that the Poles could not be described as a nation following their partition.[73] This is simply not true in al-Husri's definition of a nation, and he stresses that a common economic life comes only after the creation of a national state; it is one of the results of the establishment of a nation, not one of the factors in its establishment.[74]

Al-Husri also attempts to diminish the significance of geographical factors as national components. He is forced to admit, however, that geography can be a meaningful secondary element because of its potentially negative role; the loss of geographical continuity can result in national division and can, with the passage of time, lead to a linguistic and historical differentiation.[75] Still, al-Husri refuses to

71 *Ma hiya al-qawmiyyah?*, pp. 163-164.
72 *Ibid.*, pp. 164-168; *al-Qawmiyyah al-'arabiyyah*, p. 81.
73 *Ma hiya al-qawmiyyah?*, pp. 170-186.
74 *Ibid.*, p. 186.
75 "'Awamil al-qawmiyyah," in *Abhath mukhtarah*, p. 53.

accept the argument that a nation must have a definite, fixed tract of land in order to be called a nation. Recalling his personal experiences prior to the Young Turk revolution of 1908, he points to the entangled Macedonian situation where one small area contained scattered groups of Bulgarians, Greeks, and Serbs. Yet because these groups preserved their own linguistic and historical traditions, they constituted nations despite their failure to possess defined geographical territory.[76]

Al-Husri also addresses himself to the problem of religion and its role in the creation of nations. Although he appreciates the powerful emotional force of religion, he finds in it a lack of uniformity in relation to nationalism. Universal religions, like Christianity and Islam for example, which are open to all, which proselytize and embrace many areas and peoples, are opposed to nationalism. These religions can create ties equivalent in strength to ties of nationalism only to the degree that they are successful in spreading a language. Usually the areas affected retain their distinct language and culture, but there are instances such as the spread of Arabic by Islam, where a new language and thus a new nationality can be adopted through a universal religion.[77] Al-Husri also identifies national religions, that is, those which restrict themselves to a particular people or locale and which can, because of their natural tie to the language and history of their area, serve as an element of nationalism. In this manner Luther's movement is regarded by al-Husri as a national as well as a religious revolt because it attempted to end the domination of the Latin lan-

[76] *Al-'Urubah bayn du'atiha wa mu'aridiha*, pp. 88-89; *Hawl al-qawmiyyah al-'arabiyyah*, pp. 101-102.

[77] " 'Awamil al-qawmiyyah," in *Abhath mukhtarah*, pp. 46-48, 51.

guage and the Latin countries in favor of a vernacular language of worship and a national church.[78]

Al-Husri points out that matters were somewhat different once the principle of nationalism came to dominate the European scene. At this time, national movements took place independently of religious considerations. This indicates to al-Husri that national unity does not necessarily follow religious unity, as witnessed by the Balkan peoples who waged war amongst themselves even though the majority were Greek Orthodox. Conversely, religious differences do not prevent the realization of national unity, as evidenced by the union of Catholic Bavaria with Protestant Prussia.[79] Al-Husri further argues that the separation of church and state in Europe occurred only after a long series of rebellions and intellectual developments which should prove very clearly to the Arabs that the independent functioning of national and religious elements in society is not a natural result of Christianity and therefore is not restricted to Christian nations.[80]

In support of this general theoretical exposition, al-Husri calls upon history as his witness. He has given examples in time from the Roman Empire to the Syrian-Egyptian union of 1958, and in space from Finland to Indonesia as evidence of the triumph of language and history and the inability of economics, religion, and will to force or deter national unity. Still, he regards the movement beginning in nineteenth century Europe with the unification of Italy and proceeding to Germany, the Balkans, and Turkey as the most valid and instructive model for the Arabs. At one point he remarks, "I will speak of the history of the rise of the na-

[78] *Ibid.*, pp. 45-49. [79] *Ma hiya al-qawmiyyah?*, pp. 197-206.
[80] *Ibid.*, p. 199.

tionalist idea with the belief that these historical studies will direct a searchlight toward our political thought and will help us to predict what the nationalist idea will be in the Arab countries."[81]

Although he is familiar with the roles of Cavour and Garibaldi, al-Husri treats in more detail German unification, which he regards as "the most important and enjoyable page of nineteenth century history."[82] There are a number of possible reasons for his more detailed examination of German than Italian unification. First, there was the obvious power differential between the two states once they achieved unity—Germany served as a more impressive example of the awesome capabilities that accrue to a unified nation than did Italy. Secondly, Italy was tainted in Arab eyes by her Libyan adventure of 1911-1913. And finally, al-Husri is somewhat disillusioned by the assistance, which he nevertheless recognizes as not wholly beneficial, rendered Italian unification by French policies.[83]

Al-Husri interprets the genesis of German nationalism as dating from the defeats at the hands of Napoleon and the subsequent recognition on the part of intellectuals and politicians that these defeats stemmed from a lack of national unity and patriotic spirit.[84] In view of the pre-existing cultural unity in Germany, he believes that the methods for achieving total national unification centered on the spread of nationalist feelings through the recognition of the shared language and history of the many German states, and the efforts to overcome the regional selfishness of those who ruled them. There was no unity of will in Germany, and the politicians and princes who sought to preserve the

[81] *Nushu' al-fikrah al-qawmiyyah*, p. 24. [82] *Ibid.*, p. 26.

[83] On this last point, see "al-'Ilm li al-'ilm," in *al-Wataniyyah*, pp. 154-155.

[84] *Nushu' al-fikrah al-qawmiyyah*, pp. 28-31.

status quo resemble the opponents of Arab unity today, just as the debates of the time resemble the debates now taking place in the Arab world over the problem of unification.[85] While al-Husri acknowledges that the *Zollverein* played some role in preparing the way for eventual German unification, he stresses that the ideologues and poets who spread the idea of nationalism created a spiritual desire for unity which was stronger and more significant than any material element.[86] And the major contributing factor to these emotions was the recognition on the part of the German people of their shared language and history.

Greece is seen by al-Husri as another example of the decisive role played by language and history in the creation of a unified national state. He concedes a significant role to religion in this instance, pointing out that Greece was the first of the Balkan countries to awaken because it preserved its language, history, and a kind of nationalist existence through the Orthodox Church.[87] But again, language, not religion, was the immediate vehicle for the Greek nationalist awakening.

Since the first independent Greek state created in 1830 failed to correspond to the borders of Greek nationality, it was only natural that the efforts of the next several decades should be devoted to the incorporation of all Greek-speaking peoples into the Greek nation.[88] This sort of Irredentism is inevitable and justifiable. Al-Husri explains, however,

[85] *Al-'Urubah bayn du'atiha wa mu'aridiha,* pp. 24-27.

[86] *Nushu' al-fikrah al-qawmiyyah,* pp. 45-53. See pp. 64-65 for the discussion of the *Zollverein.* Making a different point in another work, al-Husri credits the *Zollverein* with a slightly more spiritual character. See *al-'Urubah awwalan* (Arabism First), 5th ed., Beirut, 1965, pp. 165-166.

[87] *Al-Qawmiyyah al-'arabiyyah,* pp. 104-108.

[88] *Nushu' al-fikrah al-qawmiyyah,* p. 78.

that the Great Idea under Venizelos failed because expansion into Anatolia had no basis in nationality.[89]

Bulgaria, on the other hand, was subject to two different oppressions prior to her nationalist awakening: first, the intrusions of the Greek Orthodox church which opposed Bulgarian national existence and sought to spread Greek language and culture among the Bulgarians; and second, the political domination of the Ottoman Empire which was not, however, opposed to the existence of a Bulgarian language.[90] Hence, Bulgaria first had to secure its national existence from the Greek Orthodox church before it could work for political independence from the Ottoman Empire. This was achieved by the revival of the Bulgarian language, the inauguration of new studies of Bulgarian history, and finally the establishment of a Bulgarian patriarchate which made the language of worship and education Bulgarian instead of Greek.[91] It was only after this national cultural independence was achieved that the movement for political independence could be undertaken.

It has been suggested that this interpretation of Bulgarian history by al-Husri is a further reflection of Ibn Khaldun's theory of the relationship between religion and *'asabiyyah* in the sense that it is a recognition that religion does not have the potential to create a national community, but only the limited ability to strengthen one which already possesses the natural solidarity based on national bonds.[92] Yet it should be emphasized that in the historical example of Bulgaria, religion to al-Husri represents national culture; he

[89] *Ibid.*, p. 83.

[90] *Ibid.*, pp. 86-87; "'Awamil al-qawmiyyah," in *Abhath mukhtarah*, p. 50.

[91] *Nushu' al-fikrah al-qawmiyyah*, pp. 88-91.

[92] Hourani, *Arabic Thought*, p. 315.

maintains that the only reason for the rivalry between Greece and Bulgaria throughout the period before World War I was language. They were of the same religion.[93]

In a similar manner, al-Husri relates the history of the Albanian and Yugoslavian national movements.[94] He is particularly impressed by the efforts of the nationalist clubs, secret societies, and armed bands which he witnessed during his eight years in the Balkans.

From his position as an Arab nationalist, al-Husri views as both necessary and natural the development of the Turkish nationalism he had once opposed. He has studied the phenomenon at some length, most notably in *al-Bilad al-'arabiyyah wa al-dawlah al-'uthmaniyyah* and *Muhadarat fi nushu' al-fikrah al-qawmiyyah.* His involvement in the early stages of the intellectual movement of which the genesis of Turkish nationalism was a part and his later concern for the subject have made his contributions of some historical significance.

Al-Husri's basic premise regarding the development of nationalism in Turkey is that it came not as a desire for political independence or national unity, but as a new awakening, as a discarding of the Ottoman and Islamic characteristics of the Empire.[95] The current of Turkish nationalism began with the Turkification of the language, moved to the Turkification of history, and culminated in the Turkification of the state.[96] According to al-Husri, the

93 *Nushu' al-fikrah al-qawmiyyah,* p. 97.

94 See *ibid.,* pp. 104-113; and *al-'Urubah bayn du'atiha wa mu'aridiha,* pp. 20-22. Al-Husri's narrative of Balkan national history is examined by Kenny in "al-Husri's Views," pp. 240-242.

95 *Nushu' al-fikrah al-qawmiyyah,* pp. 116-122; also, *al-Bilad al-'arabiyyah wa al-dawlah al-'uthmaniyyah,* pp. 20-28, for a discussion of the Islamic nature of the Ottoman Empire.

96 *Nushu' al-fikrah al-qawmiyyah,* p. 127.

movement for Turkifying the language and the historical emphasis on the role of the Turks in pre-Islamic times helped disseminate the feeling of Turkish nationalism and enabled it to capture the hearts of the Turkish people. Once recognized, this trend was irreversible and, in association with the abolition of the caliphate in 1924, left only nationalism as a source of inspiration and identification. By thus institutionalizing nationalism, it could be used in implementing reforms such as the removal of the veil when it was argued that women once played an important role in ancient Turkish life, or in language when it was considered necessary to free Turkish from Arabic and Persian influences.[97]

Al-Husri has high praise for Atatürk, admiring his policies in recruiting the material and moral forces of the people to eliminate the Greek invasion and, of equal significance, his adherence to national frontiers determined by language and history.[98] Al-Husri also clearly approves of the abolition of the caliphate. Atatürk, then, provides him with an example of an effective Middle Eastern leader who mobilized his people and sustained his nation through the force of nationalism. To initiate a similar reorientation in the Arab lands was a fundamental objective of al-Husri's work.

Theories and Models Applied: The Arabs as a Nation

An account of al-Husri's general analysis of nationhood in the West has been presented because it forms the basis

[97] *Ibid.*, pp. 150-151. Al-Husri has chosen to ignore the incomplete nature of the Turkish transformation and instead overemphasizes the influence of nationalism and secularism.

[98] *Al-Qawmiyyah al-'arabiyyah*, pp. 111-118.

for his more specific views. The arguments with which he defends his position on Arab nationalism are expressed with the conviction that the inexorable force of history will prove him correct. His is not a treatment of civilization in general with theories on its rise and fall, but a consciously formulated selective interpretation of modern history designed to meet a specific situation. The concentration on episodes of national unification provides what he feels is irrefutable historical evidence for his statements regarding the nationhood of the Arabs. He conceives of a direct lineal connection between the process of European and Arab history, and the events which history has unfolded will repeat themselves in the Arab lands.[99]

Within the framework of al-Husri's interpretation of history, the sharing of language, and to a lesser extent history, is the essential determinant of Arab nationhood. All countries whose inhabitants speak Arabic are Arab countries, no matter how numerous the states which govern them, no matter what flags fly from their government buildings, and no matter how crooked the boundaries which divide them politically.[100] Defined in these terms, the Arab countries

[99] The notion of a lineal historical connection is suggested by Kenny in "al-Husri's Views," p. 235. Al-Husri concluded his *Lectures on the Growth of the Nationalist Idea* with the declaration that of all the various trends extant among the Arabs at the present time, the greatest influence would be exerted by nationalism. "We can be absolutely certain of this," he continued, "on the basis of studies on the history of nationalism in general." *Nushu' al-fikrah al-qawmiyyah*, p. 239.

[100] *Al-'Urubah awwalan*, p. 11. German nationalists of the nineteenth century often employed the same criterion. Arndt, for example, in his poem *Das Deutschen Vaterland*, asked "What is the fatherland of the German?" and then replied: "The whole of Germany it must be. As far as the German mother-tongue sounds." Quoted in Ergang, *Herder*, p. 173. The development of Arab attitudes toward their language as a national and cultural source is discussed in Anwar G. Chejne, *The Arabic Language*, Minneapolis, 1969, pp. 16-19, 21-24.

stretch "from the Zagros Mountains in the East to the Atlantic Ocean in the West, from the shores of the Mediterranean and the foothills of Anatolia in the North to the Indian Ocean, the sources of the Nile, and the great deserts in the South."[101] Language is the ultimate criterion for membership in these countries, and anyone who speaks Arabic and is located in them is an Arab, irrespective of his religion, ethnic background, family history, or official citizenship.[102] Because of the bond of language, these countries and their inhabitants are not separate and unrelated. They have been defined as Arab, and *"al-'arab ummah wahidah"* (the Arabs are one nation).[103] As for that nation, neither will nor economics, neither blood nor religion, neither its present political division into numerous states nor its past subjection to foreign rulers can deny its existence or prevent its future unity.

Since language is such an essential element in his call for Arab unity, al-Husri has little sympathy for colloquial Arabic. He regards it as a divisive factor, and certainly the existence of various dialects among the Arab regions weakens his argument on the unity of the Arabic language and hence of the Arab nation. Shortly after his arrival in Iraq in 1921, he became involved in a discussion on the subject during a dinner party at the house of Miss Gertrude Bell, the noted British observer of Arab affairs. Those present claimed that the existing relationship between classical Arabic (*al-'arabiyyah al-fusha*) and colloquial Arabic (*al-'arabiyyah al-'ammah*) was similar to that between Latin and French.[104] Al-Husri strongly opposed this contention, but he has nevertheless recognized and endeavored to minimize the differences between classical and colloquial

101 *Al-'Urubah awwalan*, p. 11.
102 *Ibid.*, p. 12.
103 *Ibid.*, p. 13.
104 *Mudhakkirati*, I, pp. 58-59.

Arabic. At one point he wrote that the Arabs must be aware of the danger involved in the spread of colloquial dialects for the divisions they created weakened national unity and facilitated the achievement of imperialist objectives.[105] In his Iraqi journal *Majallah al-tarbiyah wa al-ta'lim* he stressed the importance of teaching classical Arabic in conversation, and he later urged a reconciliation between colloquial and a simplified classical which would make the latter easier to learn.[106]

Al-Husri also feels there is an occasional misconception concerning the word Arab itself, noting that some believe it refers only to uncivilized Bedouins and is thus an unworthy term of identification. Al-Husri was led to correct this view in explicit statements that language rather than occupation or life style distinguishes an Arab. He explains: "It has been proven that the word Arab is not limited to Bedouins and the inhabitants of the desert or to the inhabitants of the Arabian peninsula. It includes all those who pronounce the *dad,* Bedouin and settled, dwellers of cities and countryside, of deserts and mountains."[107]

A certain degree of qualification is required for al-Husri to substantiate his claim that the broad geographic area and diverse peoples he has defined as Arab actually have a

105 "Al-Isti'mar wa al-ta'lim" (Imperialism and Education), *al-Risalah,* IV, no. 137 (1936), p. 255. See also Chejne, *Arabic Language,* p. 166.

106 "Al-Lughah al-fusha fi al-muhadithat" (Classical Arabic in Conversations), *Majallah al-tarbiyah wa al-ta'lim,* I, no. 5 (1928), pp. 265-268; *Durus fi usul al-tadris* (Studies on the Principles of Teaching), II, 4th ed., Beirut, 1948, pp. 122-126; *Ara' wa ahadith fi al-lughah wa al-adab* (Views and Discussions on Language and Literature), 2nd ed., Beirut, 1966, pp. 40-46. Hereafter *al-Lughah wa al-adab.*

107 *Al-'Urubah bayn du'atiha wa mu'aridiha,* p. 124. See also *Mudhakkirati,* II, p. 67; "Dawr Misr fi al-nahdah al-qawmiyyah al-'arabiyyah" (The Role of Egypt in the Arab National Awakening) in *al-Wataniyyah,* pp. 144-145. This essay orginally appeared in the Baghdad newspaper, *al-Bilad,* in 1936.

shared history. No nation, he states, has ever known true historical unity throughout its entire existence. It is therefore explained that unity of history should be understood as "the comparative, general unity which manifested itself in the most important pages of history, the pages which produced the basic culture of the nation, gave it its present language, and stamped it with its special characteristics. . . ."[108] Even approached in this manner, al-Husri's notion of Arab historical unity is something of an idealized exaggeration. In the end, it would seem that language is the most fundamental natural unifying factor for the Arab nation. History can, however, play a leading role in inspiring national sentiments.[109]

The necessity, naturalness, and inevitability of Arab unity as well as al-Husri's own identification with this cause are demonstrated in the following statement from a lecture delivered in Damascus in 1944:

> I am one of those who believe in Arab unity with a deep faith, and one of those who say that it is a duty to work unceasingly in its cause. I firmly believe that Arab unity is "necessary" in order to preserve the existence of the Arab peoples and that it is "natural" in relation to the life of the Arab nation and its long history. I have no doubt that it will be realized some day. I do not know if I will be allowed to live until that day. However, I say in all sincerity that if I do live until the day on which Arab unity is realized, I shall consider myself the happiest of all people, I will forget all the pain and hardships I have suffered, and I will leave this life gladly.[110]

108 " 'Awamil al-qawmiyyah," in *Abhath mukhtarah*, p. 54.

109 Kenny rightly questions Hourani's assertion that to al-Husri language is the only objective basis of the nation by pointing out al-Husri's belief in the motive force of selected national history. See "al-Husri's Views," pp. 243, 254; Hourani, *Arabic Thought*, p. 313. The use to which al-Husri puts history will be discussed below, pp. 141-148.

110 "Al-Istiqlal al-thaqafi" (Cultural Independence), in *Hawl al-wah-*

As was the case among the nations of Europe, explains al-Husri, the Arab nation has no bonds which supersede those of language and history. When the editor of the Cairo-based magazine *Ruz al-Yusuf* claimed that Egypt and Iraq would eventually unify because of interests other than those relating to the Arab character of each country, al-Husri replied that there would be no such interests at all if Egypt and Iraq did not share the same language and the same long history. Discounting both religion and geography, al-Husri claims that Egypt has more in common with Iraq than with Muslim Turkey or geographically proximate Ethiopia.[111]

The same arguments are used in dealing with the problem of will. Anyone who speaks Arabic is an Arab, whether he is aware of it or not, whether he wants to be an Arab or not.[112]

To eliminate religion as a basic focus of personal loyalty and identification in the predominantly Muslim Middle East and to subordinate it to the linguistic and historical ties of secular nationalism constitutes a delicate undertaking.[113] Al-Husri embarks on just such a task, however. He does so by distinguishing Arab from Islamic history. It was

---

dah al-thaqafiyyah al-'arabiyyah (On Arab Cultural Unity), Beirut, 1959, pp. 106-107. It is rare for al-Husri to deal with his personal hardships so openly. It may be a rhetorical device for added emphasis, or it may be truly symptomatic of what was undoubtedly a difficult period in his life following his expulsion from Iraq in 1941.

111 *Al-'Urubah awwalan*, pp. 166-167. Al-Husri is replying to an article which appeared in the magazine in December 1953. It was written by Ihsan 'Abd al-Quddus.

112 "Al-Qawmiyyah al-'arabiyyah," in *al-Qawmiyyah al-'arabiyyah*, pp. 65-66.

113 The conflicts and confusion embodied in this transition are discussed in Leonard Binder, *The Ideological Revolution in the Middle East*, New York, 1964. See esp. chaps. II, IV, V.

in much the same way that the Christian Arabs first presented evidence for their cultural identification with an Islamic-oriented society.[114] Al-Husri seeks to affirm this identification while diminishing the Islamic orientation of Arab society in general. He carries the arguments of al-Kawakibi, Muhammad 'Abduh, and Rashid Rida concerning the Arabness of Islam to a secular conclusion without attempting to debate the theological problems with which these thinkers were concerned.

He emphasizes the advanced, purely Arabic civilization which existed in the Arabian peninsula before the advent of Islam. Evidence for the sophistication of the civilization rests with its language. The *qasidas* and the Quran include words which convey abstract meanings and indicate a high level of intellectual achievement in pre-Islamic Arabia.[115] They also confirm the existence of the Arabic language, and hence the Arab nation itself, prior to Islam.[116] This heritage belongs to all Arabs and is one of which they can be proud.

It is acknowledged that the appearance of Islam drastically altered the course of Arab history and provided the motive force for the conquests which spread the religion and expanded the area of Arab nationality.[117] What al-Husri selects for emphasis in this regard is the intense nature of the Arabization process in some areas and its simultaneous limits when it confronted strongly entrenched

114 Among them were Nasif al-Yaziji and Butrus al-Bustani. See Antonius, *Arab Awakening*, pp. 45-54.

115 *Ma hiya al-qawmiyyah?*, p. 252; *al-Lughah wa al-adab*, pp. 247-248.

116 Cf. Hourani, *Arabic Thought*, p. 315. Al-Husri's implicit assumption that the language of the Quran was drawn from the intellectual environment of the time raises the question of whether or not he regards it as divinely inspired, as a work of God. It is most likely that he does not, further demonstrating his secular outlook.

117 *Ma hiya al-qawmiyyah?*, pp. 252-257.

national cultures in other areas. Al-Husri thus continues to distinguish between Arab and Islamic history. He points out that while the Arabic language was adopted as the language of life and religion by certain segments of the conquered people who did not embrace Islam, they were nevertheless the recipients of the common tie of language and assumed Arab nationality. There were, on the other hand, peoples like the Persians and later the Turks who adopted the Islamic religion but retained their own language; they thus remained outside the Arabization process and preserved their own national history, literature, and identification.[118]

Al-Husri assigns to Islam a seminal role in relation to Arab nationality, but even this is more of a concession to language than to religion. During the centuries of political fragmentation and cultural decline which the Arab world experienced, the Arabic language was in danger of breaking up into mutually unintelligible dialects. But the unchanging, mutually understood language of the Quran kept classical Arabic intact and facilitated its resurrection during the period of the modern awakening.[119] In view of the tie between nationality and language, al-Husri feels that Islam helped to preserve Arab nationality.

But this does not mean that Islam and Arab nationalism are bound together. Recent history has demonstrated to al-Husri that Islam has, in fact, been primarily responsible for the slow development of Arab nationalism. Thus, the Ottoman conquests of the Arab territories in the sixteenth

118 *Ibid.*, pp. 253-255; *al-'Urubah awwalan*, pp. 186-189. He further distinguishes between what he regards as Islamic literature, like the *Shahnama* of the Persian, Firdawsi, and purely Arabic literature to which he contends that both Christian and Muslim have contributed significant works. See *al-Lughah wa al-adab*, pp. 251-255.

119 *Ma hiya al-qawmiyyah?*, p. 255.

century are explained by the Arabs' willingness to submit to authorities who called themselves servants and protectors of Islam.[120] Yet the net result of this submission was the confining adherence to a fallacious concept of caliphal authority transmission. Al-Husri attempts to show through historical documentation that the legend concerning the transfer of the caliphate from the last Abbasid caliph, Mutawwakil, to the Ottoman sultan, Selim I, and from him to the house of 'Uthman, is untrue.[121] But true or not, Muslim Arabs submitted to the spiritual authority of the Ottoman caliph and the Arab national awakening was retarded as a result. The Arab intellectual awakening of the nineteenth century should have been accompanied by a comparable nationalist movement. Instead, it was confronted with a religious reaction claiming that nationalism differed from the laws of Islam and that it was the duty of all Muslims to obey the caliph.[122] Caliph and sultan were one and sought to stamp out the power of nationalism by substituting Turkish for Arabic in the Arab schools and administration.

It was for this reason that Arab nationalism was initiated by forces not directly subject to the religious authority of the caliph.[123] The first significant events which shook this authority were the Wahabbi uprising in Nejd and Muhammad 'Ali's revolt against the sultan. Al-Husri admits that

120 *Al-Bilad al-'arabiyyah wa al-dawlah al-'uthmaniyyah*, pp. 40-41; *Nushu' al-fikrah al-qawmiyyah*, pp. 160-161.

121 *Al-Bilad al-'arabiyyah wa al-dawlah al-'uthmaniyyah*, pp. 42-46. Other scholarship has also proved the caliphate transfer false. See "Khalifah," by T. W. Arnold, in *The Encyclopaedia of Islam*, 1st ed.

122 *Ma hiya al-qawmiyyah?*, pp. 207-208.

123 A detailed account of al-Husri's historical narrative of this period is found in Kenny, "al-Husri's Views," pp. 246-248. See also *al-Bilad al-'arabiyyah wa al-dawlah al-'uthmaniyyah*, pp. 97-136.

neither of these movements was based on nationalism, but he feels that the founding of a modern state in Egypt under Muhammad 'Ali prepared the way for an Arab literary and intellectual awakening.[124]

More directly associated with the growth of Arab nationalism was the role performed by the Christian Arabs in Greater Syria and Iraq during the last half of the nineteenth century. The Christian Arabs, because they had no religious attachment to the caliph, regarded Ottoman rule as foreign and reacted to it on a nationalist basis impossible for the Muslim Arabs at that time. They also acquired special sectarian organizations and privileges which were denied the Muslims. In addition, their contact with the Christian West allowed a more intensive penetration of European intellectual influences.[125] Missionary activities gave a further impetus to the literary awakening through the use of Arabic in all spheres of religious activity among the Christian Arabs. This brought a response from certain Orthodox Arabs who complained about their Greek-speaking clergymen and their Greek rituals. Then, in 1889, a Syrian Arab was appointed Orthodox Patriarch of Antioch and al-Husri regards this as the first real victory of Arab nationalism.[126]

From this movement there arose a realization on the part of the Christian Arabs of the pre-Islamic achievements which then allowed Christian and Muslim Arabs to recognize their common linguistic and historical identity, to join in demands for reform, and ultimately to initiate a truly Arab revolt "free from the bonds of Islamic Ottomanism."[127]

[124] *Nushu' al-fikrah al-qawmiyyah,* pp. 159-160.

[125] *Ibid.,* pp. 161-162, 165-166; *al-Bilad al-'arabiyyah wa al-dawlah al-'uthmaniyyah,* pp. 95-96.

[126] *Nushu' al-fikrah al-qawmiyyah,* pp. 169-171.

[127] *Ibid.,* p. 219.

In the final analysis, religion failed to keep apart those who were naturally bound by ties which transcended religion:

> Arabism was not in the past nor is it in the present restricted to any sect or religion. The cooperation between Arab compatriots, in spite of the difference in their religions, was a strength in the past just as it was in the modern Arab awakening. . . . Therefore, we should be concerned with spreading the spirit of cooperation among different sects, and showing them that they are brothers and that it is their duty to place nationalist goals above sectarian considerations.[128]

As would be expected from his more general treatment of national components discussed above, economics do not occupy a primary position in al-Husri's arguments on Arab nationalism and unity. He does maintain, as he did for European nationalism, that economic diversity such as that which exists between Lebanon and Syria for example, does not negate the possibility or desirability of nationhood or political union. He also calls for economic unity, but believes it is incumbent for national political unity to precede it.[129]

As with European nationalism, Arabism has its base in emotive rather than material foundations. One is first simply an Arab because one was born as such without thinking of benefits or disadvantages. Similarly, Arabism itself is a matter of feeling and emotion, like a child's love for its mother.[130]

Al-Husri believes that these objective definitions based on the facts of history show that the Arabs constitute a

[128] *Al-'Urubah bayn du'atiha wa mu'aridiha*, pp. 124-125. Al-Husri is quoting from what he considers the favorable conclusions reached by the First Arab Cultural Congress held in Lebanon in 1947.

[129] *Al-Qawmiyyah al-'arabiyyah*, pp. 79-80; *al-'Urubah awwalan*, p. 133.

[130] *Al-Qawmiyyah al-'arabiyyah*, pp. 84-87.

nation on the same bases as the nations of Europe—language and history. Yet mere definition is insufficient. Arab unity, although inevitable because natural, will be immeasurably delayed unless a program is formulated to hasten the recognition of the foundations of this unity.[131] As has been shown, al-Husri's vision of the value of nationalism is as a catalyst in the course of modern history; and the continuity of history demands that it perform a similar role among the Arabs also. Thus, the sentiments which sparked national movements in Europe must be aroused in the Arabs. Will alone may not create nations, but the will for unity based on the proper factors of identification must be stimulated:

> Every person who speaks Arabic is an Arab. Everyone who is affiliated with these people is an Arab. If he does not know this or if he does not cherish his Arabism, then we must study the reasons for his position. It may be a result of ignorance—then we must teach him the truth. It may be because he is unaware or deceived—then we must awaken him and reassure him. It may be a result of selfishness—then we must work to limit his selfishness.[132]

Al-Husri's efforts to combat these enemies of Arabism, his proposals to teach, to awaken, and to discipline the Arabs in order to make the unification of their nation, as he has defined it, a reality, will be considered in terms of his elaboration of a new national consciousness committed to progress and change.

131 *Al-Muhadarah al-iftitahiyyah,* p. 19.

132 "Al-Qawmiyyah al-'arabiyyah," in *al-Qawmiyyah al-'arabiyyah,* pp. 65-66.

CHAPTER

4

Arabism First: The Call for Unity

Opponents of Unity: Imperialism and Regionalism

It has been suggested that the growth of pessimism, negativism, and cynicism was the principal characteristic of the Arab nationalist movement between the two world wars.[1] Certainly, articulate Arab opinion in this period found a constant source of bitterness in the division and occupation of Arab territories by Britain and France. Imperialist machinations were blamed for the failure of a unified Arab nation to emerge from the Arab revolt. As a result, the inter-war Arab independence movements, whether particularist or broadly national, were couched in anti-Western slogans. Indeed, even after independence was achieved, imperialist plots were frequently seen lurking behind the breakdown of internal programs.

Al-Husri, for his part, approaches the problem of Western influence from two interrelated viewpoints. On the one hand, he does not hesitate to identify the imperialists as

1 Nuseibeh, *Ideas*, p. 55; Khadduri, *Political Trends*, pp. 21-23.

enemies of Arabism and their ambitions as the principal cause for the division of the Arab nation into separate states following World War I. His vocabulary includes such phrases as *al-matami' al-isti'mariyyah* (imperialist greed) and *musawamat al-duwwal al-ajnabiyyah* (the bargainings of foreign states). To the extent that al-Husri employs this type of rhetoric to stimulate an Arabism based on reactions to outside influences, he assumes the Arab nationalist posture of emotional hostility to the West.

On another level, however, al-Husri's anti-imperialist statements form a vital rational ingredient for his overall theories on language and history; for, in order to sustain the argument that the Arab nation is a natural entity, he must show that intrusive rather than inherent factors have denied that nation its rightful unity. Thus, while he often criticizes Western actions toward the Arabs, his discussions are usually presented in terms of carefully constructed historical arguments which seldom lose themselves in vituperative rhetoric. And his conclusions are always the same: there are no fundamental differences among the Arabs which require that they be divided into separate states. His attention in this regard is focused primarily on the eastern Arab states of Syria, Iraq, Jordan, Lebanon, and Palestine which were carved out of the former Ottoman provinces.[2]

Al-Husri's manner of approaching this subject seldom varies. He traces, often in great detail, the diplomatic policies of the Great Powers in the years immediately preceding and following the First World War. He then explains

[2] Al-Husri has also examined and condemned the role of French and Italian imperialism in North Africa. See *al-Bilad al-'arabiyyah wa al-dawlah al-'uthmaniyyah*, pp. 153-193. His special concern with the question of Egypt is treated below.

that those policies rather than historical or linguistic differences among the Arabs themselves have caused the division of the Arab nation. A typical example is the following excerpt from a speech delivered in Cairo in 1950:

> There is left no room to doubt that the division of the Arab provinces into several states took place because of the bargaining and ambitions of the foreign states, and not according to the views and interests of the people of the countries. So, too, were the borders of these states determined by the wishes and agreements of the foreign powers, and not according to the natural demands of the situation or the requirements of indigenous interests. . . . Is it possible for us to consider, for example, the peoples of Syria as forming a true nation, different from the people of Iraq and Lebanon? Never, gentlemen. All that I have explained indicates clearly that the differences we now see between the people of these states are temporary and superficial. . . . We must always assert that the Syrians, Iraqis, Lebanese, Jordanians, Hejazis, and Yemenis all belong to one nation, the Arab nation.[3]

Al-Husri also emphasizes that the presence of imperialism is not in accordance with the natural processes in the Arab world. He mentions that some people use the examples of eastern and southeastern Europe to show that the dissolution of empires naturally produces many states. According to al-Husri, naturalness in that area of the world was not the simple fact that several states were created out of the Ottoman and Austro-Hungarian Empires, but the fact that they were all national states which grouped together people who spoke the same language. On the other hand, "it was totally unnatural (*ma kan min al-tabi'i abadan*) that there sprang from it [the Ottoman Empire] several Arab

[3] "Al-Qawmiyyah al-'arabiyyah," in *al-Qawmiyyah al-'arabiyyah*, pp. 57-58. See also *al-Bilad al-'arabiyyah wa al-dawlah al-'uthmaniyyah*, pp. 247-249; *Nushu' al-fikrah al-qawmiyyah*, pp. 225-228; *al-'Urubah bayn du'atiha wa mu'aridiha*, pp. 11-15.

states like Iraq, Syria, and Jordan with one language."[4] This proves to al-Husri that the foreigners have disrupted the natural order of things through the imposition of their own material interests.

Although al-Husri unhesitatingly describes imperialism as an enemy of Arab unity, he does not strive to create xenophobia from this description. Rather, he seeks the affirmative realization that the Arabs are naturally one nation. He refrains from articulating Arab nationalism solely as a response to external factors. To be sure, defeat can operate among the Arabs as it did in Germany after the battle of Jena by demonstrating the need for unity and for patriotic sentiments.[5] Illustrative of this process is a statement that the Arabs lost the battle of Palestine, not despite the fact that they were seven states, but rather because of it. Thus, the Palestine defeat should serve as a catalyst to force the Arabs to examine themselves and their needs, and to assist them in the realization that unity is a sacred duty.[6]

[4] *Al-'Urubah bayn du'atiha wa mu'aridiha*, pp. 19-23. The quotation is from p. 23. Particularly irritating to al-Husri in this respect is the case of Jordan. He frequently cites it as an example of the unnatural character of the imperial creations. See the same source, pp. 11-15; "al-Qawmiyyah al-'arabiyyah," in *al-Qawmiyyah al-'arabiyyah*, pp. 55-56; *al-'Urubah awwalan*, pp. 26-29.

[5] He illustrates this point by showing that Fichte and Arndt were practitioners of an uncommitted cosmopolitanism until the battle of Jena awakened their spirit of patriotism. See "Bayn al-wataniyyah wa al-ummumiyyah," in *al-Wataniyyah*, pp. 82-83. Cf. Kohn, "Arndt," pp. 787-788; and his "The Eve of German Nationalism," pp. 257-259, 265-269.

[6] *Al-'Urubah awwalan*, pp. 148-149. Al-Husri does not treat the Palestine issue as exhaustively as certain other Arab nationalists do. He does not stress the final battle or dwell on Israeli atrocities. His is a more subtle method; he constantly states the inevitability of Arab unity, including Palestine. He clearly perceives his own role in the liberation of the territory as one of propagandist rather than as a planner for direct action. In a report to the Bludan Conference, he

Nevertheless, his dislike of Western actions did not lead al-Husri to blind hatred nor to a condemnation of imperialism as the exclusive cause for the continuing division of the Arab nation. He directs his attention inward as well, identifying among the Arabs themselves certain regional doctrines which have inhibited the spread of Arabism and the achievement of unity. Al-Husri has treated regionalism at some length, but his most enduring concern with this problem has centered on Egypt. In his opinion, Egypt's lack of participation in the Arab nationalist movement prior to Nasser's revolt constituted one of the primary internal barriers to Arab unity.

One of al-Husri's first experiences after joining the Arabs was to witness the 1919 revolt in Cairo against the British.[7] He expected the Egyptians would then join with the rest of the Arabs in a nationalist campaign for independence and unity. Yet, until Nasser's policies after the 1952 revolution brought an official declaration of Egypt's Arabness, Egypt isolated herself from the general Arab nationalist movement and was in turn ignored by the majority of other Arab nationalists. Al-Husri was never able to accept this isolation. Between the two world wars, and even into the middle 1950s, he carried out an intense propaganda campaign centering on three main themes: first, that Egypt is an Arab country; second, that Egypt should, in fact, be the leader of the Arab world; and third, that it is untenable for the

---

suggested a program to counter Zionist claims through the dissemination of information to the West, to the East, and to the coming generation of Arabs which would face the greatest threat from Zionism. This report, written in 1937, is reproduced as "Hawl al-qadiyyah filastin" (Concerning the Palestine Problem) in *Mudhakkirati*, II, pp. 469-473.

[7] Al-Husri had gone to Cairo to collect educational materials for his work in Syria under Faysal. See above, p. 58.

Egyptians to have primary bonds of loyalty to, and identification with, any ideology other than Arabism.

At their inception, these were unique arguments, initiated during a period when Egypt was seeking its own identity within either an Islamic religious context or on the basis of a non-Arab secular heritage. Egypt was regarded neither by its leaders nor the rest of the Arab world as primarily an Arab country.[8] Al-Husri's stand on the question of Egypt clearly demonstrates the broad horizons of his Arabism and his concern for an all-inclusive unity. Only one who was not deeply rooted in Arab society, who was unaffected by political considerations or regional attachments, could propose such a new and uncompromising reorganization of loyalties.[9]

With a sweeping historical presentation, al-Husri supports his contention that Egypt has been an integral part of

[8] In an interview with the author on September 28, 1966, al-Husri recalled an Egyptian who had told him that Egypt wanted no Arabs and no leadership. Officially, at least, this attitude changed substantially—in December 1963 al-Husri was publicly decorated in Cairo by Nasser for services to the cause of Arab nationalism. For the various efforts of Egypt to seek its own distinct cultural personality, see Marcel Colombe, *L'Évolution de l'Égypte 1924-1950*, Paris, 1951, pp. 167-173; Safran, *Egypt in Search*, esp. pp. 125-180. On Egypt's exclusion from various inter-war plans for Arab unity, see Haim, *Arab Nationalism*, pp. 45-51. A clear analysis of the political and intellectual currents surrounding Egypt's isolation from and gradual support of Arabism is found in Anwar G. Chejne, "Egyptian Attitudes Toward Pan-Arabism," *The Middle East Journal*, XI, no. 3 (1957), pp. 253-268.

[9] He also deplores the Hashimite-Sa'udi rivalry in the manner of the unaligned, cutting across all considerations other than those of unity. See *al-'Urubah awwalan*, pp. 48-51. A refutation of Lebanese regionalism is contained in an essay delivered to the Arab Cultural Club in Beirut in the late 1940s, "Thaqafah al-'arabiyyah wa thaqafah al-bahr al-abyad al-mutawassit" (The Culture of Arabic and the Culture of the Mediterranean Sea), in *Hawl al-wahdah al-thaqafiyyah al-'arabiyyah*, pp. 109-133, esp. pp. 120-133.

the Arab world since the first conquests. During the time of the Umayyads and Abbasids, he portrays the country as part of a great Arab empire which stretched from Central Asia to the West Coast of North Africa.[10] Under the Fatimids, Ayyubids, and Mamluks as well, various parts of Syria, Hejaz, and North Africa are described as lying within the borders of Egypt. Al-Husri points out that in more recent times Muhammad 'Ali was not only the ruler of Egypt, but that he controlled Greater Syria and areas of Hejaz too.[11] This unity of history has led to unity of language and culture and establishes beyond all doubt that Egypt is an Arab country.[12]

But Egypt is not simply an Arab country; it is the most outstanding of them. In an essay of 1936 entitled "Dawr Misr fi al-nahdah al-qawmiyyah al-'arabiyyah" (The Role of Egypt in the Arab National Awakening), al-Husri explains: "Nature has endowed Egypt with every characteristic and advantage which prescribes as a duty its assumption of the leadership in the awakening of Arab na-

10 Al-Husri is aware of the argument that Egypt gained its independence from the Abbasids during the reign of the Tulunids. He makes this seem insignificant, however, by arguing that the frontiers of Egypt at that time extended to the whole of southern Syria. See "al-Qawmiyyah al-'arabiyyah," in *al-Qawmiyyah al-'arabiyyah*, p. 63. Al-Husri is correct in his geographical designation of Tulunid domains, although the dynasty (868-905) was a successful attempt to break away from the Abbasid caliphate. See "Tulunids," by H.A.R. Gibb in *The Encyclopaedia of Islam*, 1st ed.

11 "Al-Qawmiyyah al-'arabiyyah," in *al-Qawmiyyah al-'arabiyyah*, p. 61. Although the Sudan is not specifically mentioned in this passage, al-Husri usually includes it as part of the Arab nation. See, for example, *al-'Urubah awwalan*, p. 112. Despite his praise for Muhammad 'Ali, al-Husri does not believe that he operated on nationalistic principles.

12 "Al-Qawmiyyah al-'arabiyyah," in *al-Qawmiyyah al-'arabiyyah*, p. 61; *al-'Urubah awwalan*, pp. 108-109.

tionalism."[13] It lies in the heart of the Arab countries and is the wealthiest and most advanced of them; it comprises the largest Arab bloc and has the longest history of having formed a modern political state. All of this makes Egypt "the natural leader" of Arab nationalism.[14] At another point al-Husri draws the full historical analogy of leadership when he states: "I am one of those who believe that Egypt has a special place in the Arab world, and I desire, with all my heart, that Egypt work for the realization of Arab unity as Prussia worked for German unity and as Piedmont worked for Italian unity."[15]

If language and history have firmly established Egypt as an Arab country naturally destined for the leading role in the Arab world, why then, in al-Husri's opinion, has it failed to respond to the cause of Arab nationalism? Partly it has been due to the country's comparative isolation from the centers of Arab nationalism—an isolation which resulted from the British occupation.[16] Equally reprehensible to al-Husri, however, has been the espousal by certain Egyptians of bonds of loyalty which conflict with the fundamental goal of Arab unity. Such doctrines have elicited a steady stream of rebuttals from al-Husri. For example, to those who say that Egypt is essentially a part of Africa, al-Husri replies that continental culture areas do not exist, and that surely Egypt has more in common with Iraq and Kuwait than with Uganda and Transvaal.[17] There are others who maintain that Egypt's identity should be based

[13] In *al-Wataniyyah*, p. 143. Cf. Haim, *Arab Nationalism*, pp. 50-51.

[14] *Al-Wataniyyah*, pp. 143-144; "Naqd nizam al-ta'lim fi Misr," in *al-Tarbiyah wa al-ta'lim*, p. 184.

[15] *Al-'Urubah awwalan*, p. 125.

[16] *Nushu' al-fikrah al-qawmiyyah*, pp. 230-231; "al-Qawmiyyah al-'arabiyyah," in *al-Qawmiyyah al-'arabiyyah*, pp. 59-60.

[17] *Al-'Urubah awwalan*, pp. 90-96.

on a general Mediterranean bond. Al-Husri responds to this view by pointing out that Egyptian ties with North Africa are strong because they are based on language and history rather than on Mediterranean culture in general. He then goes on to argue in his usual manner that Egypt is bound more strongly to all other Arab countries than to Greece, Italy, and Spain.[18]

Al-Husri also objects to religious ties because they interfere with national loyalties. His comments on this subject will be treated in detail below. As far as Egypt is concerned, his principal contention is that because not all Egyptians are Muslims, nationalism based on linguistic and historical affinities rather than religious sentiments ought to bind them together.[19]

Arousing further concern on al-Husri's part were the attempts of certain Egyptian intellectuals to articulate a distinct modern Egyptian cultural identity based on the Pharaonic heritage. Especially heated in this respect were his exchanges with Taha Husayn in the late 1930s.[20] Al-Husri sharply opposed Taha Husayn's arguments as they were expressed in *Mustaqbil al-thaqafah fi Misr* (The Future of Culture in Egypt) to the effect that Egypt was part of Europe in character and temperament while at the same time the country retained its distinctive identity through a Pharaonic core.[21] Al-Husri was prompted to reply that by

[18] *Ibid.*, pp. 97-99.

[19] *Ibid.*, pp. 100-101.

[20] Taha Husayn (b. 1889) in an active, controversial, and much-honored career as literary critic, educational reformer, translator, and novelist, has become the dean of modern Egyptian letters. He has been the subject of a literary biography by Pierre Cachia, *Taha Husayn*, London, 1956. See also Hourani, *Arabic Thought*, chap. XII; Safran, *Egypt in Search*, pp. 129-131, 175-179.

[21] See al-Husri's critiques under the general title "Hawl kitab mustaqbil al-thaqafah fi Misr" (On the Book *The Future of Culture in Egypt*), in *al-Risalah*, VII, nos. 316-321 (1939). Taha Husayn's book

ignoring the role of language, Taha Husayn failed to distinguish what was truly unique in Egyptian culture. In a series of sarcastic questions included in an article written in 1938, al-Husri asked if Husayn's statement on the penetration of Pharaonic feelings into the hearts of the Egyptians meant that the language, civilization, and religion of the Pharaohs should be restored.[22] How could Dr. Husayn ignore the course of history which has shown conclusively the Arabness of Egypt? The Pharaonic epoch is buried under time and Egypt cannot reject living Arabism on the pretext of identification with a dead civilization. Could a modern Egyptian communicate more easily with a revived mummy or with Ibn Khaldun? The pyramids do not deny the fact that Egypt speaks the same language as the rest of the Arab countries. Arab nationalism does not demand the destruction of the ancient Egyptian monuments or the elimination of pride in them. But Egyptians must realize that they are Arabs first, and that their primary loyalties should be to the Arab nation.[23]

Similar remarks appear throughout al-Husri's works. They all lead to a common, ringing conclusion of which the following is typical:

> Arabism is the strongest and most important of the ties which bind Egyptians to each other. This is because all Egyptians, whether they are Muslim or Christian, from Upper or Lower Egypt, speak Arabic. . . . We can therefore be certain that

---

has been translated by Sidney Glazer, *The Future of Culture in Egypt*, Washington, D.C., 1954.

22 "Bayn Misr wa al-'urubah: kitab maftuh ila Dr. Taha Husayn" (Between Egypt and Arabism: An Open Letter to Dr. Taha Husayn), in *al-Wataniyyah*, pp. 122-123. This essay originally appeared in the journal *al-Risalah*, VI, no. 285 (1938).

23 *Ibid.*, pp. 123-126; *al-Qawmiyyah al-'arabiyyah*, pp. 90-91, 127; *al-'Urubah awwalan*, pp. 113-114.

> Egypt is Arab and that its future will be bound by the strongest of ties to Arabism.[24]

When this is realized, as it must be, "then the Egyptians will join with the sons of the other Arab countries in saying: 'Arabism above and beyond all else.' "[25]

By thus defining and debating the problems of regionalism, al-Husri brings into perspective his concept of Arab unity.[26] If countries recognize their Arabness, then they will surely realize that they should be unified. Al-Husri applauds as important first steps the institutionalization of Arabism in the constitutions of various Arab states.[27] In addition, initially he saw in the formation of the League of Arab States a hopeful sign of approaching Arab unity. From one of his most cherished dreams, however, the Arab League became one of his greatest disappointments. Three years after its formation in 1945, he called it a living organism, nourished and strengthened by the spirit of Arabism.[28] Yet, by 1951 he condemned the League as the institutionalization of regionalism, not Arabism, and as an organization devoted to petty political activities rather than to the propagation of nationalism.[29]

[24] *Al-'Urubah awwalan*, pp. 113-114. [25] *Ibid.*, p. 113.

[26] He has also taken issue with Antun Sa'adah, not on the basis of Sa'adah's reforms or his general nationalist policy, both of which al-Husri approves, but over the regional nature of his doctrines. See *Difa' 'an al-'urubah* (A Defense of Arabism), Beirut, 1956, pp. 15-63; and *al-'Urubah bayn du'atiha wa mu'aridiha*, pp. 70-138. An excellent account of Sa'adah's doctrines and his party is found in Zuwiyya-Yamak, *Nationalist Party*.

[27] *Al-Qawmiyyah al-'arabiyyah*, pp. 7-11.

[28] *Safahat min al-madi al-qarib*, pp. 104-105.

[29] *Al-Qawmiyyah al-'arabiyyah*, pp. 31-32; *al-'Urubah bayn du'atiha wa mu'aridiha*, pp. 140-147; *al-'Urubah awwalan*, pp. 152-153. Particularly vitriolic in this respect are al-Husri's criticisms of what he regards as the Egyptian regionalist policies of 'Abd al-Rahman al-'Azzam,

According to al-Husri, these barriers to Arab unity can be overcome through the recognition of affirmative forces. It is in this realm that al-Husri's efforts have been directed ever since he adopted Arab nationalism. He does not conceive the basis of Arabism as a negative reaction to external disasters or to internal political and ideological quarrels. To do so would destroy the concepts of the process of history and natural nationhood around which he has constructed his arguments for unity. He thus refuses to accept the argument put forth by the Egyptian historian, Shafiq Ghurbal, to the effect that Arabism is simply the result of European imperialism. In rejecting Ghurbal's premise, al-Husri distinguishes between Arabism itself and the awareness of its existence. Arabism, al-Husri maintains, had its beginnings in the remote past and existed because the Arabic language existed. While he admits that the recognition and expression of Arabism are of recent origin, he believes that it continues to be a natural manifestation of linguistic ties rather than an artificial response to imperialism.[30] Instead of negativism and pessimism, then, al-Husri attempts to provide his vision of Arabism with a positive internal dynamic.

This dynamic is generated and sustained by spiritual and emotional factors which are the basic components in al-Husri's efforts to implement Arab unity. For example, when he was asked to provide specific details for the creation of unity, he simply replied:

> I believe that in the present circumstances, the first action that must be taken to realize Arab unity is to awaken the feelings

---

the first Secretary General of the Arab League. See *al-'Urubah awwalan*, pp. 68-73, 116-126.

30 *Al-'Urubah awwalan*, pp. 185-186. Al-Husri is discussing an article by Ghurbal which appeared in the January 1, 1955 issue of the journal *al-Hilal*.

> of Arab nationalism and to spread faith in the unity of this nation. When these feelings are completely awakened and when this faith is thoroughly spread and firmly established in the people, then the path for Arab unity will become clear and the obstacles which oppose it will vanish easily.[31]

But by what means is this awareness to be spread? How is this faith to be implanted and maintained? For al-Husri, the solution lies in a particular type of education. Realizing that his generation suffers from the uncertainty of formulating a new doctrine and from the bitterness of seeing its plans frustrated by external intervention and internal dissent, al-Husri places his hopes for the future on the proper education of the Arab youth. From the reorganization of Darülmuallimin in Istanbul in 1909 to his educational work in Iraq, Syria, and the Institute of Higher Arab Studies, he regarded education as the most effective instrument for the creation of a dedicated citizenry and a progressive society. Like Pestalozzi, Herder, and Fichte, by whom he has been influenced in this matter, al-Husri believes strongly in the value of national education—national both in emotional orientation and inclusive scope. Fichte, for example, saw the remedy for Prussia's defeat by Napoleon in the complete regeneration of society through the educational system.[32] Al-Husri echoed these sentiments in an Arab context in an essay of 1932 in which he stated that the goal of education could not be the preservation of Arab society as it then existed, but must center on making the younger generation active in the creation of a new society.[33] In his

[31] *Ibid.*, p. 5.

[32] See G. H. Turnbull, *The Educational Theory of J. G. Fichte*, Liverpool, 1926.

[33] "Ahamm masa'il al-tarbiyah" (The Most Important Questions of Education), in *al-Tarbiyah wa al-ta'lim*, p. 144. Fichte wrote the following on this general subject: "By means of the new education we want

practice of modern pedagogical methods, al-Husri combined a concern for the improvement of general educational standards with efforts aimed at making the classrooms a seedbed for Arab nationalism. It was not enough, in his opinion, simply to prepare the students intellectually; they must have ingrained in them a nationalistic pride, an understanding of national objectives, and the spiritual characteristics required to serve these objectives. He writes: "We must therefore concentrate our educational efforts on directing the new generation toward the goal which we ultimately seek: the unification and advancement of the Arab nation."[34] Al-Husri's belief in the leading role played by education in the inculcation and implementation of nationalism must be kept in mind during the following discussion of his attitude toward history, Islam, and internal reform.

The Value of History

An essential ingredient in al-Husri's system of national education is the direction of certain elements in the educational process along preconceived lines which will increase faith in the desirability and possibility of unity. Thus, while

---

to mould the Germans into a corporate body, which shall be stimulated and animated in all its individual members by the same interest. . . . So there is nothing left for us but just to apply the new system to every German without exception, so that it is not the education of a single class, but the education of the nation. . . ." Fichte, *Addresses*, p. 15. But where Fichte saw the new education as deeply involved with divine precepts and extending to all humanity, al-Husri rejects the divine and confines the objectives of education to the more immediate context of achieving Arab unity. Cf. Turnbull, *Educational Theory*, p. 80; Fichte, *Addresses*, pp. 38-41.

34 "Ahamm masa'il al-tarbiyah," in *al-Tarbiyah wa al-ta'lim*, p. 144.

he admits the acceptability of the phrase "knowledge for the sake of knowledge," he maintains that it is incorrect to infer from this that teaching is also simply for the sake of teaching.[35] It is within this context that his full utilization of history is most clearly demonstrated.

The importance which al-Husri attaches to history as an essential element of nationhood and as a justification for his belief in unity has already been shown. By defining history as the feelings and consciousness of a nation, he logically believes that historical studies can be utilized as a driving force capable of spreading and sustaining the faith needed to promote unity.[36] Al-Husri indicates that this functional importance of historical studies has been recognized by imperialist nations. He points out that whenever such nations conquer another nation, they immediately try to consolidate their military takeover with spiritual control, the most important aspect of which is the direction of the spread of historical knowledge to the younger generation.[37] The results of such external control over the dissemination of a nation's history are viewed by him as disruptive:

> We find that the national feeling among subject nations starts to diminish and then becomes extinguished when forgetfulness spreads its wings on the national history, especially when a nation turns from its own history to a "history" that has been falsified by the ruling authorities.[38]

This is particularly relevant in relation to the Arab nation

35 "Al-'Ilm li al-'ilm," in *al-Wataniyyah*, p. 147.

36 For an examination of various recent Arab views of history, including al-Husri's, see Anwar G. Chejne, "The Use of History by Modern Arab Writers," *The Middle East Journal*, XIV, no. 4 (1960), pp. 382-396, esp. pp. 390-394. See also Kenny's discussion in "al-Husri's Views," pp. 253-254.

37 "Al-'Ilm li al-'ilm," in *al-Wataniyyah*, p. 151; "Bayn al-madi wa al-mustaqbil," in *ibid.*, p. 111.

38 "Al-'Ilm li al-'ilm," in *al-Wataniyyah*, p. 151.

whose history has been perverted by the anti-Arab bias contained in work done by Western historians, and by the heavy reliance of certain Arab historians on Western sources.[39] Discussing this last point, al-Husri contends that the fierce struggle which continued for many centuries between East and West has resulted in a spiritual estrangement between the two cultures. He further believes that this struggle has given the West an unfavorable view of Orientals in general and of Arabs in particular. This bias is manifested in studies which find Westerners "withdrawing from neutrality" when they write about the Arabs.[40]

In order to eliminate the influence of this bias and to achieve national unity, the full force of national history must be recognized and utilized. As interpreted by al-Husri, it is a most dynamic force:

> We do not exaggerate when we say that the movements for resurrection and the struggles for independence and unity begin only by recalling the past and searching for revelation from history. . . . Love of independence is nourished by memories of the lost independence; the longing for power and glory begins with a lament for the lost power and glory; faith in the future is derived from a belief in the brilliance of the past; and the longing for unification is increased by the renewal of memories of the past unity.[41]

[39] "Ahamm masa'il al-tarbiyah," in *al Tarbiyah wa al ta'lim*, pp. 146-147.

[40] *Ibid.*, p. 147; "al-'Ilm li al-'ilm," in *al-Wataniyyah*, pp. 156-157. For an example of what he regards as a biased approach, see his review of the last two volumes of Jacques Pirenne's *Les Grands Courants de l'Histoire Universelle* in *The Middle East Journal*, XIII, no. 2 (1959), pp. 201-204. It is asserted that Pirenne has made numerous factual errors in his statements on Arab history and that his opinions reflect political prejudice and a lack of objectivity in matters concerning the Arab world.

[41] "Al-'Ilm li al-'ilm," in *al-Wataniyyah*, p. 152; also, "Bayn al-madi wa al-mustaqbil," in *ibid.*, pp. 111-112. Germany, Greece, Turkey, and

Because the past is capable of such restorative and inspirational powers, the Arabs must review their own history from a nationalistic point of view and apply it in their educational system. Al-Husri firmly declares that history is the most valuable and useful educational tool available to teachers for the promotion of patriotic and nationalistic sentiments, and "we therefore consider it a duty to adopt historical studies as the core of national education."[42]

This requires the practice of a selective historicism with clearly defined objectives and thus represents a departure from the methodology of detached historical research. As Rupert Emerson has remarked, "What is cherished in the national myth may not only be shot through with inspired fiction but must also inevitably be a somewhat arbitrary selection from the multiplicity and perversity of the age-old

---

Serbia are mentioned as outstanding examples of nations which have recognized and acted successfully on this knowledge. The following remarks by a noted political scientist are especially relevant to al-Husri's statement just quoted: "In the face of towering uncertainties, a new historical consciousness is needed. Everywhere the spokesmen of nascent nationalism must fight against the humiliation of the recent past—invasion by older nations, colonial or dynastic imperialism, princely or tribal fragmentation. Everywhere they must seek to enlist energies for a difficult and hazardous task. Their most persuasive argument is that what once was can surely be again. The glories of a remote past—real or mythical—become the allies against the immediate past in the struggle for a better future." Dankwart A. Rustow, *A World of Nations*, Washington, D.C., 1967, p. 43.

42 "Ahamm masa'il al-tarbiyah," in *al-Tarbiyah wa al-ta'lim*, p. 146; also "Ta'lim al-ta'rikh wa al-'alaqat al-duwwaliyyah" (The Teaching of History and International Relations), in *Ara' wa ahadith fi al-ta'rikh wa al-ijtima'* (Views and Discussions on History and Society), 2nd ed., Beirut, 1960, pp. 29-30. Hereafter cited *al-Ta'rikh wa al-ijtima'*. The essay cited was originally delivered as a lecture to the First Arab Cultural Congress in 1947.

record."[43] Al-Husri never admits directly the necessity of employing fiction, maintaining that while some nations have benefited from fabricated historical legends, the Arab nation has no need to do so because its past truly abounds in glorious deeds.[44]

What is required, therefore, is selection, the kind of forgetting mentioned by Renan in his "Qu'est ce qu'une nation?" speech: "The essence of a nation is that all the individuals have many things in common, and also that they have all forgotten a good many things."[45] Al-Husri argues that since the very complexity of history forces the teacher to select only a limited number of facts for classroom presentation, this selection should be carried out so as to deepen the spirit of nationalism in the souls of the students.[46] To al-Husri, this means ignoring the black pages of the past, for they negate the spiritual vitality of which history is capable and weaken students' faith in the future.[47] All nations have experienced periods of decline, but these need not be introduced into the classroom.

[43] Rupert Emerson, *From Empire to Nation*, Boston, 1966, p. 149. Similar observations are made with specific references to Arab nationalism in Nuseibeh, *Ideas*, pp. 77-84.

[44] Al-Husri adds that as far as the Arabs are concerned, accentuation and modification are sufficient to provide the nationalist orientation. He further states that he believes in pure historical research, but does not want to see it introduced into the classroom under the divisive conditions which presently prevail in the Arab world. See "al-'Ilm li al-'ilm," in *al-Wataniyyah*, pp. 153, 157; "Ta'lim al-ta'rikh wa al-'alaqat al-duwwaliyyah," in *al-Ta'rikh wa al-ijtima'*, pp. 45-46. Cf. Kenny, "al-Husri's Views," pp. 245, 253-254.

[45] Renan, *Discours*, p. 286. Renan specifically urged Frenchmen to forget the St. Bartholomew massacres of the sixteenth century.

[46] "Ahamm masa'il al-tarbiyah," in *al-Tarbiyah wa al-ta'lim*, p. 146; "Ta'lim al-ta'rikh wa al-'alaqat al-duwwaliyyah," in *al-Ta'rikh wa al-ijtima'*, p. 46.

[47] "Al-Iman al-qawmi" in *Abhath mukhtarah*, p. 104.

Al-Husri has no doubt that the Arabs have known greatness in the past, although he creates no specific national myth except in his call that the historical unity of the Arabs is something great in itself and should serve as the basis for unity in the future. He also stresses the achievements of Arab men of science and letters who contributed to the course of human civilization while Europe languished in the dark ages. One can detect a certain defense mechanism at work here. He must show that the greatest periods of Arab history have never been inferior to those of the West, and that, in fact, there were times when the Arabs were far more advanced than the West.[48] It should also be noted that al-Husri continues to display Arab greatness in secular terms. He does not offer a defense of Islamic civilization. Language created the bond which has given historical continuity to Arab unity; both language and history will, then, provide the bonds for unity in the future.

By approaching history in this manner, al-Husri justifies his insistence that Western secular national movements should be carefully studied to provide inspiration in what he envisages as a similar future for the Arabs in relation to nationalism. He laments the fact that the Arabs received their initial historical and political knowledge from France and England alone. The development of nationalism among the Arabs would have taken place more rapidly if the movements in Italy, Germany, and the Balkans had been studied in depth.[49] Al-Husri has legislated against this gap by including specific directions in the Iraqi elementary school curriculum of 1922-1923 requiring that sixth-year history

[48] *Ibid.*, pp. 104-109; "Hawl al-qati'ah al-madi" (On Severing the Past), in *Abhath mukhtarah*, p. 435. This latter essay was originally published in 1928 in *Majallah al-tarbiyah wa al-ta'lim.*

[49] *Al-Muhadarah al-iftitahiyyah*, pp. 14-16.

classes concentrate on unification movements, especially the policies of Cavour and Garibaldi in Italy and of Bismarck and the Hohenzollern family in Germany.[50]

To ensure that the entire history program was implemented along nationalistic lines, al-Husri issued rigorous directives to history teachers in Iraq. The following instructions accompanied his elementary school curriculum of 1922–1923 and illustrate the closed emphasis of his national educational policies:

> The basic goal of historical studies in elementary schools is to teach the history of the fatherland and the past of the nation. The ultimate objective to be derived from this is the strengthening of patriotic and nationalistic feelings in the hearts of the students. Therefore, the history of Iraq and of the Arab nation should be the core of historical studies. As for the history of other countries, it should not be studied in the first courses except as it relates to the history of Iraq and of the Arabs. . . . The idea of the unity of the Arab nation and the Arabism of Iraq should be brought out clearly from the beginning.[51]

Thus, al-Husri believes that by the utilitarian employment of a judiciously selected history, Arab youth can be mobilized for the achievement of national goals.

He notes that the use of history in this manner is regarded unfavorably by some who consider it characteristic of modern dictatorships.[52] He vigorously supports his position, however, arguing on the grounds of history and practicality. All nations, he maintains, have benefited by subjecting history to the demands of nationalism. It may be

[50] *Mudhakkirati*, I, p. 216.

[51] *Ibid.*, pp. 215-216. See further pp. 475-480, for al-Husri's reports to teachers for the academic year 1924-1925. These reports are also on nationalistic education and echo the same principles as the instructions quoted in the text. Other examples are cited from different sources in Chejne, "The Use of History," pp. 391-394.

[52] "Al-'Ilm li al-'ilm," in *al-Wataniyyah*, pp. 152-153.

true that this is no longer necessary in the majority of European countries where nationalism has already been used to provide the impetus for independence and national unification. Such is not the case, however, in the countries of the East, especially among the Arabs, where nationalism has not yet completed its task.[53] Since other nations have proven that the proper use of historical studies plays an important role in spreading national feelings, the entire matter can be justified from a purely functional viewpoint: "We believe that our need for the utilization of history in patriotic and nationalistic education exceeds that of all other nations without exception."[54] The essence of al-Husri's concern is national awareness leading to national unification. Until these twin objectives have been achieved, all else is irrelevant. If the use of history to increase nationalist sentiments contains the seeds of militant nationalism, it also possesses the capabilities of creating unity out of division, and herein lies its primary importance for al-Husri.

The Problem of Islam

Because of the positive, all-embracing nature of his nationalist ideology, al-Husri cannot escape a certain conflict with Islam. Islam itself is a self-contained sense of identity, a basis from which to view the world and around which to organize society. As has been shown, the initial Ottoman and Arab responses to manifestations of Western superiority were evolved within the context of Islam.[55] A

[53] *Nushu' al-fikrah al-qawmiyyah,* pp. 22-23.

[54] "Al-'Ilm li al-'ilm," in *al-Wataniyyah,* p. 156.

[55] The Christian Arabs were naturally an exception. Even among them, however, the contact with the West was frequently based on religious affiliation. The sympathy of Europe was with them because they were Christians who, in turn, looked to Europe for protection.

purified or reformed Islam was seen as the vehicle through which self-respect could be restored and the foreigner rejected. To the degree that Islam and nationalism are able to coincide in opposition to the outsider, they are essentially compatible and, frequently, essentially negative. The crucial problem with regard to al-Husri's doctrines is that a society can understand and unite against an obvious material danger more readily than it can focus on a positive, spiritual reorientation to achieve a distant and little understood goal.[56]

Al-Husri's ideology of Arab nationalism is based on the positive, organic forces of language and history more than on the negative rejection of foreign occupation, although this latter is certainly the object of his deep frustration and anger. In addition, he calls for a substantial reformulation of the basis of Arab loyalty and identity. The conflict between this view and the one which defends Islam as a civilization and religion under attack is increased by the basically secular nature of his personal beliefs. Indeed, nowhere is his ambivalent relationship to Arab society more evident than in his confrontation with Islam.

Al-Husri's arguments for a separate consideration of Islamic and Arab history and his views on the caliphate as a barrier to the development of Arab nationalism have

[56] This dichotomy between a constructive nationalism seeking to evoke a positive loyalty to society and a religiously oriented nationalism founded on rejection of the alien is suggested by Wilfred Cantwell Smith in his *Islam in Modern History*, New York, 1959, pp. 81-83. As Smith writes on p. 82, "It is easier to see what one is or should be fighting against than to imagine what one is or should be fighting for." He goes on to argue that a positive nationalism urging a new form of existence is, in his opinion, much less common among the Arabs than a negative-based religious nationalism. Cf. H.A.R. Gibb, *Modern Trends in Islam*, Chicago, 1947, pp. 115-120, where the tendency for Islam to assimilate nationalism is also discussed.

already been discussed. Three additional aspects of his involvement with Islam will be examined here: first, his attitude toward the continuing propaganda for Islamic unity; second, the extent to which he seeks an accommodation between Islam and Arab nationalism; and finally, his assumption that a secular reorganization of Arab society is desirable.

Can the inspiration that was once achieved by loyalty to Islam be transferred to the plane of a positive secular nationalism? This is a crucial question for al-Husri. He obviously believes that such a transfer should take place and attempts to show that it is urgently required. The identification of Arabism with Islam must be diminished immediately. If Islam once performed a valuable role by preserving the classical Arabic language, it now threatens, in the age of nationalism, to be a factor of dispersion and divisiveness. Arab nationalism is no longer tied to Islam in immediate linguistic or historical terms: "We must recognize before all else that we are living in an age which has, for a long time, separated political connections from religious ones."[57] How, he asks, can one argue for Islamic political unity in the light of the linguistic and cultural differences which exist among the various Muslim nations? Do those who do so see the folly of calling for unity between Fez, Cairo, Hyderabad, and Tehran before unity between Cairo, Baghdad, Damascus, Mecca, and Tunis is completed? Islamic brotherhood and mutual cooperation represent one thing, but political union between various Muslim countries is quite something else, and al-Husri asserts his belief in the impossibility of such a union.[58] His essential

[57] *Al-'Urubah awwalan*, p. 101.

[58] "Bayn al-wahdah al-islamiyyah wa al-wahdah al-'arabiyyah" (Be-

objection to one type of unity and his affirmation of another rests, as usual, with language. He asks how one can hope for creation of the unity of Islamic countries which speak different languages without the creation of unity among countries which speak one language and therefore constitute one nation.[59] There was an Arabic language before there was Islam, and the loyalties embodied in that language are presently owed to the Arab nation, not to Islam. What the Arab revolt showed us we should never forget, al-Husri admonishes, Christian and Muslim Arab have the same language, the same long history, and an overlapping literature and culture, all of which make them a part of each other in a way which was never possible for the Balkan peoples and which never will be possible for the Islamic peoples.[60] Al-Husri concludes that propaganda for Islamic unity diverts efforts away from the goal to which all attention should be devoted: the achievement of Arab unity.

Only the tortured Palestine problem caused al-Husri to

---

tween Islamic Unity and Arab Unity), in *al-Wataniyyah,* pp. 98-99. This essay constitutes al-Husri's most eloquent and forceful examination of the problem of Arab versus Islamic unity. It originally appeared in the journal *al-Risalah,* VII, no. 328 (1939) and has been translated by Haim in *Arab Nationalism,* pp. 147-153.

59 "Hawl al-wahdah al-'arabiyyah" (On Arab Unity), in *al-Wataniyyah,* pp. 138-139. This essay originally appeared in the journal *al-Risalah,* VII, no. 315 (1939). See also "Radd 'ala tasrihat Shaykh al-Maraghi" (A Reply to the Statements of Shaykh al-Maraghi), in *al-Wataniyyah,* pp. 171-172. Shaykh Mustafa al-Maraghi was a reforming rector of al-Azhar in the 1930s. His negative attitude toward Arabism was expressed by his call for the realization of Islamic unity without the consideration of Arab unity. See Colombe, *L'Égypte,* p. 172.

60 *Nushu' al-fikrah al-qawmiyyah,* pp. 217-218.

depart from the consistency of his normal stand on religion. In two articles written in 1937 and 1938 he stated the need to direct propaganda to all the Muslims of the world in order to arouse their support for the Arab struggle against Zionism.[61] His elaboration of the usefulness of religious ties placed him in an unfamiliar posture and his arguments in this instance were contrived and unconvincing. By pointing out that one's sympathy toward any natural disaster affecting thousands of people was contingent upon the closeness of the relationship to the afflicted, al-Husri attempted to lay the groundwork for a statement that the entire Islamic community was involved in the Palestine question and its sentiments should be awakened by a call to Islamic brotherhood. But his arguments became diluted with respect to Islam when he appealed in the same sentence to the general considerations of human rights and justice, and eventually concluded that a strictly Arab concern for Palestine should be greater than that of any other group.[62] Even in this isolated plea to Muslim sentiment, al-Husri could not in the end include religious ties in other than a superficial manner.

With his secular background and long familiarity with Western history where he believed the separation of church and state made possible the restructuring of society along national lines, al-Husri was equipped to take such a stand. Neither education nor inclination forced Islam into his life in personal terms. Within the society of which he was a member, however, Islam intruded everywhere upon his concept of nationalism. For this very reason, he could not

61 "Hawl al-qadiyyah filastin" in *Mudhakkirati,* II, pp. 469-473; and "Hawl al-wajib al-dini wa al-wajib al-qawmi tijah filastin" (Concerning Religious and National Duties toward Palestine), *ibid.*, pp. 473-475.

62 "Hawl al-wajib al-dini," pp. 474-475.

explain away Islam, he could not pretend that it did not exist and still claim the loyalties of people predominantly Muslim. In order to alleviate potential hostility to his version of Arabism, he therefore had to demonstrate that Islam and nationalism were not mutually exclusive. His method was a technical and unemotional one. Haim points out that all Arab nationalists must somehow accommodate their doctrines to Islam. She is less convincing, however, in her claim that al-Husri's efforts to demonstrate the compatibility of Islam and nationalism constitute one of the major thrusts of his nationalist ideology. Such an argument gives undue emphasis to what is, on al-Husri's part, a begrudging concession to religion in order to further nationalism.[63]

To argue, as some do, that nationalism is irreligious and demands the abolition of religion is, in al-Husri's opinion, to misunderstand the true nature of nationalism. He suggests that the French word *laïque*, which he defines as *non-religieux* or *non-clerical* rather than *irreligieux*, is a more suitable description of the relationship of nationalism to religion.[64] Scientists, army leaders, and politicians work and study in their own special fields independent of religion, but this does not make them irreligious. In the same manner, nationalism and nationalists are not irreligious. Al-Husri's argument does, however, implicitly underline the separation of religion and nationalism.

Moreover, his statements on the assistance Arab unity can

63 Cf. Haim, *Arab Nationalism*, pp. 53-58; and the more secular interpretation of al-Husri's message in Khadduri, *Political Trends*, p. 204. See also the discussion by Ibrahim Abu-Lughod on the need for ideologies in the Arab world to function within the dimensions of emotional attachment to Islam in "Retreat from the Secular Path? Islamic Dilemmas of Arab Politics," *The Review of Politics*, XXVIII, no. 4 (1966), pp. 447-476.

64 *Al-'Urubah awwalan*, p. 177.

give to Islamic unity, while clever, fail to convince one that he truly accepts any partnership between religion and nationalism. He puts the Islamic unionists in a position which makes them appear to oppose the very objective they seek:

> The idea of Islamic unity is broader and more inclusive than the concept of Arab unity. It is impossible, then, to advocate Islamic unity without also advocating Arab unity. We are therefore correct in asserting that he who opposes Arab unity opposes Islamic unity as well.[65]

He asks that the scholars of Islam not neglect the demands of reason and logic; if they maintain their belief in the possibility of realizing Islamic unity, they must at least admit that efforts to achieve Arab unity constitute one stage on that path.[66]

Thus, the point of contact between al-Husri's doctrine of Arab nationalism and Islam is a slight one. He attempts to channel the beliefs of the Islamic unionists into support for Arab unity, but never does he place Arab nationalism at the service of Islamic unity. In one of his replies to Taha Husayn, he assures the Egyptian that however much he believes in the idea of Arabism and the possibility of Arab unity, he believes with equal depth in the impossibility of Islamic unity.[67] Nearly twenty years later, his position remained unchanged: "I, personally, am one who calls for the unification of the Arab countries without believing in the possibility of unifying the Islamic countries. I do, however, believe in the necessity of religious reforms."[68] This is as far as al-Husri ever goes in affirming his own religion or his

65 "Bayn al-wahdah al-islamiyyah wa al-wahdah al-'arabiyyah," in *al-Wataniyyah,* p. 100.

66 *Ibid.,* p. 104.

67 "Hawl al-wahdah al-'arabiyyah," in *al-Wataniyyah,* pp. 139-140.

68 *Al-'Urubah awwalan,* p. 181.

belief in the desirability of Islam operating in association with Arab nationalism. It is a most qualified affirmation. He can assert his Arabism, but not his belief, either personal or societal, in institutionalized religion.

This position is reflected in his praise for the work of 'Ali 'Abd al-Raziq who advocated the abolition of the caliphate on the grounds that the historical evidence for its required existence as an Islamic religious institution was insufficient. 'Abd al-Raziq further contended that religion was a private spiritual matter between the individual and God, not to be regulated by the laws of the state.[69] Al-Husri himself welcomed the abolition of the caliphate by Atatürk and felt that it forced the Arabs, and especially the Egyptians, to look at themselves in national rather than religious terms.[70] Al-Husri does not deny that one can be a Muslim, or a Christian for that matter, and a loyal nationalist at the same time. But he asserts the primacy of secular nationalism in all spheres of modern Arab life, stating that this doctrine should receive the loyalties of the individual in pursuing the task ahead—the realization of Arab unity. His attitude is summarized in his espousal of the phrase *al-din li Allah wa al-watan li al-jami'* (religion is a matter between the individual and God while the fatherland is the concern of all).[71]

69 'Ali 'Abd al-Raziq (b. 1888) was an Egyptian *'alim.* His attack on the caliphate appeared in his controversial book published in 1925, *al-Islam wa usul al-hukm* (Islam and the Principles of Government). As a result of his stand, he was dismissed from his position as an *'alim* and a judge in the *Shari'ah* courts by the governing body of al-Azhar University. See Hourani, *Arabic Thought,* pp. 189-192; Khaldun S. al-Husry, *Three Reformers,* Beirut, 1966, pp. 120-125. Sati' al-Husri's examination of al-Raziq's ideas is found in *Ma hiya al-qawmiyyah?,* pp. 242-247.

70 "Dawr Misr fi al-nahdah al-'arabiyyah al-qawmiyyah," in *al-Wataniyyah,* p. 145.

71 *Al-'Urubah awwalan,* p. 101.

Al-Husri's romanticism is not based on a belief in a higher power spreading earthly progress, but on historical evidence which has proved linguistic nationalism successful in unification efforts. He believes in man's ability to shape his own environment and is very much the skeptic when confronted with statements such as the one made by Dr. Ahmad Zaki that God's will was directing mankind toward one international community.[72] Al-Husri was exposed to the scientific method and positivist doctrines from his earliest school days in Istanbul. His first career was that of a natural science teacher during which he was influenced by French literature on the subject rather than by the debates of Muhammad 'Abduh or the Ottomans of pan-Islamic persuasion. Moreover, he had experienced the inability of religion to serve as a satisfactory force of unification in the Ottoman Empire. He has therefore articulated another form of identity based on his understanding of Western history. In addition, his own identification would have been incomplete had it been expressed solely in Islamic terms. True, his background in Arabism was not very strong either, but it was at least an ideology which he could intellectually support.

He avoids theological debates, refrains from any mention of the bygone purity of Islam or its present adaptability to the modern world, and in general conveys the impression of the secular man forced to deal with a necessary evil which cannot be totally dismissed without provoking a violent and self-defeating reaction. His arguments are never supported with Quranic citations or phraseology, and the

[72] *Al-Qawmiyyah al-'arabiyyah*, pp. 128-129. Zaki's statement was made in an article in the journal *al-Misri*.

poetry he most often quotes is from the secular work of his Ottoman friend Tevfik Fikret.[73]

This position was not unrecognized by his critics. An anecdote which appeared frequently in the Baghdad newspapers during the 1930s portrayed al-Husri and several intellectuals discussing various matters in al-Husri's huge library which contained volume after volume dealing with every imaginable subject. When the topic of conversation switched to a religious matter, however, it proved impossible to find a Quran with which to settle the debate.[74] The story is apocryphal (al-Husri owned several Qurans) but serves to illustrate the attitude held toward him.

It is therefore evident that al-Husri increases the significance of secular nationalism at the expense of Islam. His objective is not to focus attention on religious reform, but to spread a desire for Arab unity, not to turn to religion for identification and emotional inspiration, but to the language and history of the nation. While tacitly recognizing the overwhelming presence of Islam in Arab society, he aims at relegating that presence to a secondary position in favor of a unity which includes all Arabic speakers. Islam can partake in the general Arab unity, but only as a personal religion, not as an agency attempting to legislate to society or to dissipate national loyalties through international ties.

By stripping Islam of all but its general morality, al-Husri hopes to place its influence on the side of the struggle for national unity. This is most clearly seen in his instructions

[73] In an early essay al-Husri used the term *jihad* (holy war), calling for a *jihad* in the cause of the nationalist awakening. This term was, however, soon dropped from his nationalist vocabulary. See "al-Iman al-qawmi," in *Abhath mukhtarah*, p. 103. On Fikret, see above, pp. 24-25.

[74] Interview with Khaldun al-Husri, October 4, 1967.

on how to teach religious studies in the Iraqi secondary schools. Viewing the existing teachers of religion as ignorant of the principles of pedagogy and psychology, and generally "deprived of culture," al-Husri nevertheless endeavored to give a new thrust to a subject which perforce had to be included in the curriculum.[75] In teaching the life of the Prophet, for example, he instructed the teachers to avoid detailed discussions of his life and to confine themselves to explanations about his love and greatness. Not content with the simple memorization of acts of devotion and Quranic verses, he further required the teachers to make certain that the students understood what they were reciting. What should be extracted from these studies, al-Husri insisted, is morality, which constitutes the most important aspect of religious belief.[76] Operating on the same principles that he did in Istanbul, al-Husri felt that if taught in this manner, religious studies could serve some useful purpose by generating a societal ethic which would make the students good citizens in the future. This was in keeping with his general reorganization of education to serve the cause of Arab unity.

[75] *Mudhakkirati*, I, p. 322. These instructions accompanied the curriculum of 1922-1923.

[76] *Ibid.*, p. 322. To denote morality, al-Husri employs the traditional term *al-akhlaq*, combining its sense of ethical behavior with the added dimension of modern civic responsibility to meet the new demands of twentieth century society. See "al-Akhlaq al-fa"alah wa al-fada'il al-ijabiyyah" (Effective Morality and Positive Virtues), in *Majallah al-tarbiyah wa al-ta'lim*, II, no. 13 (1929), pp. 42-50; and his discussion of the historical evolution of morality in society in *Ara' wa ahadith fi al-'ilm wa al-akhlaq wa al-thaqafah* (Views and Discussions on Science, Morality, and Culture), Cairo, 1951, part I. Al-Husri dealt with this term in a similar manner during his Ottoman service. See Ülken, *Tarihi*, I, pp. 278-279; and also R. Walzer, "Akhlaq," in *The Encyclopaedia of Islam*, 2nd ed.

The Iraqi Minister of Education at the time, Rida al-Shabibi, criticized the changes al-Husri was making in the educational system and pointed out that young people were beginning to say that the religious sciences were obsolete. Al-Husri's reply raised the troubling, perplexing question to which he, himself, could only answer in the negative: is every Eastern tradition worth maintaining?[77] In raising this question, he faced a problem which he then had to examine—the dilemma of preserving the national heritage while at the same time reshaping society to meet the modern world.[78]

Internal Regeneration: Solidarity and Sacrifice

The manner in which al-Husri uses the past to create national awareness and pride has been examined. His general disregard for the institutions of Islam has also been noted. This cultivation of certain aspects of the Arab heritage and the disavowal of others are both conditioned by their potentialities for producing Arab unity. It is with a similar view to its benefits for unity that al-Husri is a firm advocate of change, of an attack on tradition which will bring the Arabs into the modern world. He also feels that the adoption of modernity is without question desirable in itself.

Thus, for all his emphasis on the glories of Arab history, al-Husri looks to a future reorientation of Arab society rather than to a restoration of the past:

[77] *Mudhakkirati*, I, p. 443.

[78] Rupert Emerson suggests that this is a problem which all nations must face. He discusses it in a sensitive manner in relation to the emerging nations of Asia and Africa in *From Empire to Nation*, pp. 151-158.

It [the past] becomes harmful if it begins to form an enticing force calling us to turn back. We cannot consider the past as a goal toward which we should direct ourselves or to which we should strive to return. But it is necessary that we make of the past a basic subject on which to rely in our path forward, that we create from it a dynamic power which will propel us toward a new future. In short, our motto in this respect should be: memory of the past with a constant striving to the future.[79]

Consistently underlying al-Husri's vision of a new future is the theme of regeneration (*al-tajdid*), a regeneration which will permit the Arabs to approach their problems unhindered by harmful traditions. He writes:

The pace of world civilization is marching rapidly. . . . It is necessary for us to recognize the obvious truth that we are now living in an age when standing still leads not only to backwardness, but also to disappearance. . . . In the future it will be impossible for any nation in the world to preserve its existence without arming itself—materially and morally—with the weapons of modern life. It is necessary that we fully understand this and begin our course resolutely and without delay. We must proceed along the path of regeneration in every field of life: material, moral, and social. Regeneration in everything: in language and literature, in education and morals, in science and the arts, in politics and culture, in agriculture, industry, and commerce. Regeneration in every place: in the home and in the school, in the village and the city, in the street and in the garden. Regeneration in every way, in everything, and in every place—that should be our general motto.[80]

Synonymous with regeneration is unity. Al-Husri views all successful national movements in this manner. Thus, a

[79] "Bayn al-madi wa al-mustaqbil," in *al-Wataniyyah*, p. 114. See also "Hawl al-qati'ah al-madi," in *Abhath mukhtarah*, p. 436.

[80] *Al-Ta'rikh wa al-ijtima'*, pp. 25-26. Similar sentiments about the demands of modernity are also expressed in "Thaqafah al-'arabiyyah wa thaqafah al-bahr al-abyad al-mutawassit," in *Hawl al-wahdah al-thaqafiyyah al-'arabiyyah*, pp. 126-130.

national awakening brings recognition of the shared language and history which, in turn, produces the drive for regeneration through unification. Once unified, nations experience a total sense of regeneration and become powerful in all fields.[81] The same is true for the Arabs; stagnation and acceptance of the present within each individual and community can only lead to the perpetuation of the external political divisiveness.

In addition, al-Husri insists that the Arabs' struggle for unification and regeneration must be in the modern terms of the twentieth century. There must be an acceptance of progress and change. There must also exist among the Arabs a conviction that they possess inherent capabilities for advancement in the modern world. European progress was due to a receptiveness to factors of change just as Arab progress must be. The Arabs are in no way inferior to the West and they must have pride in their own ability to achieve greatness. With this belief al-Husri opposed Salamah Musa's contention that the Egyptians, Syrians, and Iraqis were related by blood to the Aryans and should therefore be called Westerners rather than Easterners.[82] Al-Husri responds with a general repudiation of blood ties per se, and then goes on to say: "I believe only in the national tie which is based on language and history, and I regard the words 'East and Eastern and West and Western' only as geographical terms."[83] He is asserting the belief that

[81] See, for example, his account of German unification in *Nushu' al-fikrah al-qawmiyyah*, pp. 27-53.

[82] Salamah Musa (1887-1959) was a leading intellectual figure in the Arab Middle East and is often regarded as the founder of Egyptian socialism. Al-Husri's response, written in 1928, is to an article published by Salamah Musa in the journal *al-Hadith*. See "Hawl al-qati'ah al-madi," in *Abhath mukhtarah*, pp. 435-436.

[83] *Ibid.*, p. 436. See also "Hawl al-wahdah al-'arabiyyah," in *al-*

the Arabs can be proud of their heritage and confident of their future without relying on contorted evidence to prove themselves tied to the West by blood.

Although there is, in his closed system of education, an attitude indicating a desire for the West to leave the Arabs alone while the process of history takes its natural course among them, al-Husri remains too much a product of European intellectual traditions to demand the complete rejection of all things Western. His very notions of progress and of the need to separate religion from the national movement testify to this belief. In addition, he emphasizes the role which modern communications can play in the process of unification.[84] Al-Husri has no problem juxtaposing Arabism and modernity: the world can be faced in both Arab and modern terms without sacrificing either. As for what will remain specifically Arab, this is naturally thought to be the language, culture, and a sense of history. The new national self-image can thus be tied both to the acceptance of change and to the preservation of the distinctly Arab national heritage without contradiction.

Yet, al-Husri is more concerned with a general spiritual regeneration leading to national awareness than he is in detailing the precise nature of change in specific programs. Any concrete reform projects he may have outside the field of education are always subordinated to the urgency of the national awakening. Thus, "I say that it is necessary to devote every effort to reform the present conditions and to eliminate injustice as quickly as possible, provided that we do not deviate in our actions and measures from the re-

---

Wataniyyah, pp. 137-140 where al-Husri states that there should be no difference between the modern Arab and modern European intellects.

[84] *Nushu' al-fikrah al-qawmiyyah*, pp. 228-229.

quirements of patriotism and that we believe at all times: the fatherland before and above everything else."[85] In his ordering of priorities, nothing must interfere with the prerogatives of nationalism.

Nor does al-Husri specify the form of government which would be the most instrumental in carrying out the desired regeneration. He steadfastly remains above the realm of politics, feeling that any entrance into this field would dilute his message of its spiritual power. He does, however, occasionally single out certain political systems in order to comment on their relationship to nationalism.

He quite naturally finds Communism and all forms of internationalism objectionable on the grounds that they disrupt the bonds of nationalism. He acknowledges the debt that the Arabs owe to the Soviet Union for its struggle against imperialism, but he cannot accept the dissolution of all national ties in order to establish new ones on the international basis of class.[86] While maintaining that he has no differences with Communism or socialism as forms of political organization, he asks that these movements not make their calls hostile to nationalism. The Arab nation has just awakened from a long sleep, its bonds of patriotism and nationalism are still weak, and any attraction to internationalism is harmful and cannot be condoned.[87]

Al-Husri's reaction to events in Mussolini's Italy was more favorable. In 1930 he wrote, "We can say that the sys-

[85] "Bayn al-wataniyyah wa al-ummumiyyah," in *al-Wataniyyah*, p. 95. The lack of a clearly defined social program in the ideology of secular Arab nationalism is discussed in general terms by H.A.R. Gibb in "Social Change in the Arab East" in Philip W. Ireland (ed.), *The Near East*, Chicago, 1942, pp. 57-58.

[86] "Bayn al-wataniyyah wa al-ummumiyyah," in *al-Wataniyyah*, pp. 89-90.

[87] *Ibid.*, p. 94.

tem to which we should direct our hopes and aspirations is a Fascist system, not a Bolshevik system."[88] This was an attraction felt by many Arab nationalists for the revival of both Italy and Germany, powers which they saw as having been dominated like themselves by England and France. It was also hoped, especially in Iraq, that assistance might be obtained from Italy and Germany against Britain and France.[89] Al-Husri was particularly impressed by what he regarded as Fascism's ability to generate mass feelings of nationalism, sacrifice, and communal solidarity.[90] At the core of his own concept of regeneration are attempts to ingrain both the habit of individual sacrifice for the nation and feelings of communal solidarity. These are recurrent themes in al-Husri's works and appear with special frequency in his essays and lectures of the 1930s. The approach may be said to be traditional in the sense that it endeavors to inculcate collective values; but in inspiration and ultimate objectives, it embodies a radical departure from tradition.

The strength of human societies, according to al-Husri, is not determined by the number of individuals which compose them, but by the strength of the ties which bind these individuals to each other. Some nations, although populous, are weak because they lack internal solidarity. The Arabs

[88] "Manhaj al-madaris al-awwaliyyah fi Rusiyyah al-Sufyatiyyah" (The Curriculum of Elementary Schools in Soviet Russia), *Majallah al-tarbiyah wa al-ta'lim*, III, no. 23 (1930), p. 82.

[89] For details on Iraqi responses to German and Italian overtures, see Hirszowicz, *The Third Reich*; Khadduri, *Independent Iraq*; and the latter's "General Nuri's Flirtations with the Axis Powers," *The Middle East Journal*, XVI, no. 3 (1962), pp. 328-336.

[90] As early as 1921 al-Husri predicted, after personally witnessing in Rome the public enthusiasm demonstrated during D'Annunzio's reading of poems on the Fiume adventure, that Italy would soon make its voice heard in world politics. *Mudhakkirati*, I, p. 31.

must avoid such an existence: "We must strive to make the parts of our beloved nation adhere firmly to each other like stone, not like sand which has a loose and brittle cohesiveness."[91] Critically examining certain aspects of modern Arab life on this basis, al-Husri finds that the Arabs exhibit individualism to a greater degree than they do communal solidarity.

He used a broad range of easily understood examples to drive home his point. In one article, he deplored the rude behavior of Baghdad theater audiences, particularly a group which responded to his request for quiet with assertions of their freedom. Al-Husri editorialized on this negative display of group interest and then observed sadly: "There is a great difference between us and Westerners in this. When they go to a theater, there is silence during the performance. They know the social obligations of each individual in a public place."[92] If the Arabs were to achieve unity, this weakness must be eliminated. Al-Husri describes the remedy as follows: "We can say that what the Arab needs first and foremost is communal education which will strengthen the spirit of solidarity, obedience, and sacrifice in his soul so that he can be successful not as an individual existing for himself alone, but as a person serving his nation as well."[93] Thus, education once again plays a critical role in the promotion of unity, this time by ordering the relationship of the individual to society and providing him with the proper communal values.

As an adjunct to civil education, al-Husri places heavy emphasis on military training as a means to instill senti-

91 *Al-Qawmiyyah al-'arabiyyah*, p. 93.

92 "Al-Tarbiyah al-ijtima'iyyah" (Social Education), *Majallah al-tarbiyah wa al-ta'lim*, I, no. 4 (1928), pp. 200-201.

93 "Ahamm masa'il al-tarbiyah," in *al-Tarbiyah wa al-ta'lim*, p. 145.

ments of communal solidarity. From the initial establishment of the British mandate, the question of conscription was a pressing one in Iraq. Iraqi nationalists felt that if they were going to achieve independence as stipulated in the mandate provisions, they should be allowed to prepare for their own defense.[94] Each rejection of conscription proposals was seen by these nationalists as a British plan to keep Iraq defenseless. Al-Husri was an ardent proponent of conscription throughout this period. When the National Service Law endorsing universal compulsory military training was finally passed in 1934, he told an audience at Dar al-Mu'allimin that he regarded the event as the most important development of the entire year in the Arab East.[95] In al-Husri's estimation, universal military conscription is as essential as compulsory education for the successful growth of a modern nation. Civil education takes the child from his family, unites him with comrades, and commits him to education in the interest of the nation. A similar function is performed by military service which removes the young man from his village, unites him with fellow countrymen, and commits him to training for the defense of the fatherland. In this sense, the military barracks can be regarded as a general educational institution like the secondary school.[96] But military life has characteristics which make it an even more valuable instrument in the service of the nation; it is a life of order and discipline, of sacrifice and altruism

[94] For the controversy surrounding conscription in Iraq, see Khadduri, *Independent Iraq*, pp. 76-77; Longrigg, *Iraq*, pp. 178-180.

[95] "Al-Khidmah al-'askariyyah wa al-tarbiyah al-'ammah" (Military Service and Universal Education), in *Ahadith fi al-tarbiyah wa al-ijtima'* (Discussions on Education and Society), Beirut, 1962, p. 44. This essay was originally delivered as a speech to the Nadi Mu'allimin in Baghdad in 1934. It is also reproduced in *al-Tarbiyah wa al-ta'lim*, pp. 68-75.

[96] *Ibid.*, p. 45.

which al-Husri summarizes in the following manner during a 1928 argument supporting conscription:

> He [the soldier] lives with a group of the sons of his fatherland who are from different towns and classes and who hold various beliefs and positions. He lives with them subject to a system in which they are all included without exception. He lives there, not with the intention of returning to his original personality or of being confined to his family and a life centered in his village. On the contrary, he works for a purpose which is loftier than all these, for a purpose which ensures the life of the fatherland and the welfare of the nation. . . . Military life makes him feel clearly the existence of nation and fatherland. He learns true sacrifice of blood and self in the cause of the nation and the fatherland.[97]

Although al-Husri does not indicate the specific military functions of the armed forces, he conceives of them as vital socializing agents within the framework of his ideas on nationalism and communal solidarity. Other organizations furthering this cause to which al-Husri gave support were the Boy Scouts and the Futuwwah youth movement.[98] He

[97] "Al-Tarbiyah al-ijtima'iyyah," pp. 208-209.

[98] The name Futuwwah stemmed from a medieval Muslim organization based on martial virtues. It was founded in Iraq in 1935 for the specific purpose of providing preliminary military training to secondary students who would then be better prepared when they served their compulsory service under the stipulations of the Law of National Defense. In 1939 membership in the Futuwwah was made compulsory for students in higher education and teachers' training colleges as well. Supported by Syrian and Palestinian nationalists in Iraq and guided by the rabid nationalism of Sami Shawkat, the Futuwwah became a popular paramilitary organization. Al-Husri's feelings toward the Futuwwah were ambivalent. On the one hand, he approved of its expansion to include upper-level students and favored the manly, nationalistic spirit which it represented. At the same time, he was disgusted with Shawkat's flamboyance and with the elaborate system of ranks, badges, and uniforms which had been

had followed closely the development of Scouting since its inauguration by Baden-Powell and regarded it as an organization which could serve to intensify the spirit of cooperation and nationalism in Iraq. Early in his term as Director General of Education he began to urge the expansion of the Boy Scouts and was eventually successful in securing the establishment of an active group.[99]

Even as he seeks to establish communal values, however, al-Husri continues to speak to the individual as well. It is necessary that each individual feel the call of sacrifice for his nation. In a lecture delivered in 1929 to a group of Iraqi army officers in the Military School, al-Husri explained that group enthusiasm was not enough and that there must be in the soul of each individual in the army strong patriotic sentiments driving him to carry out his important duty.[100]

Al-Husri feels that those nations which fail to develop or to sustain these values cannot survive. The course of modern history provided him with an example from which he issued a stern warning. In 1941 he delivered a lecture to the Muthanna Club in Baghdad entitled "*Hawl inhiyar Faransah*" (On the Fall of France).[101] In this lecture, he contrasted France's heroic World War I performance with her

---

extended to the civilian employees of the Ministry of Education. Al-Husri treats the founding and regulations of the organization in *Mudhakkirati,* II, pp. 381-387; see also, Khadduri, *Independent Iraq,* pp. 166-168.

99 *Mudhakkirati,* I, pp. 231-237; II, p. 380. The opposition of some to the movement was deeply rooted—one man told al-Husri that the three-fingered salute of the Boy Scouts represented the Christian trinity and therefore denied the absolute oneness of God central to Islam.

100 "Al-Akhlaq al-fa"alah wa al-fada'il al-ijabiyyah," p. 49.

101 The lecture is reproduced in *Safahat min al-madi al-qarib,* pp. 31-59 and summarized in *Mudhakkirati,* II, pp. 501-507.

recent stunning defeat, and the solidarity that emerged in 1914 with the political and moral division which presently existed. He conceded German military superiority in the current conflict, but denied that it was the central factor in France's quick collapse. Of more crucial significance in al-Husri's analysis was the increase in the diseases of factionalism and individualism to such a point in France that they dominated over the patriotic and communal spirit.[102] Anti-Fascist and anti-Nazi propaganda in France so belittled the New Order, the resurgent spirit of solidarity in Germany and Italy, that the French began to consider their own strength in terms of the freedom of individual thought and conscience which they possessed. This individualism continued after the outbreak of war and led to the collapse of France.[103]

Al-Husri then directed his attention inward and demanded that the events in France serve as a reminder to the Arabs. In particular, he urged the Arab youth to take full note of this historical lesson; it was, after all, their generation in France which subordinated social solidarity to unlimited individualism and so brought their nation to its present disaster.[104] It is clear to al-Husri that the individual must give himself to the nation if he and his nation are to survive. To what he regards as the disparate individualism of the Arab, he opposes the collectivism of national sacrifice. The extent of this sacrifice and the ultimate attitude to be ingrained by education and military service are indicated in the closing sentences of the lecture on the fall of France:

> I wish it realized that freedom is not an end unto itself, but is a means to a higher life. The patriotic interests which may

102 *Safahat min al-madi al-qarib,* p. 51.

103 *Ibid.,* pp. 51-52.

104 *Ibid.,* pp. 58-59.

sometimes demand a person to sacrifice his life and soul, may also demand the sacrifice of his freedom. He who does not sacrifice his personal freedom in the cause of his nation's freedom when the situation demands it, may then lose his personal freedom along with the freedom of his nation and his fatherland. He who does not consent to "lose" (*yufnī*) himself in the nation to which he belongs, may then be "absorbed" (*al-fanā'*) by a foreign nation which could someday conquer his fatherland. Therefore, I say continuously and without hesitation: "Patriotism and nationalism above and before all else, even above and before freedom."[105]

Sylvia Haim has contributed some suggestive comments on this passage. She feels that it invests, in a secular context, a religious significance to the relationship between the individual and the political group. She points out that al-Husri's word for "lose" (which should be *afnā, yufnī*) was previously used by Islamic mystics to indicate the union of the worshipper with the Godhead and that this passage is thus al-Husri's contribution to the "genuine metaphysic of nationalism."[106] Although this, like her other observations, provides illuminating insight, it seems that at another point Miss Haim endows this single passage with undue significance and constructs from it a philosophical system for al-Husri which obscures his ultimate objective of awakening nationalism in order to achieve Arab unity.[107] Furthermore, her in-

[105] *Ibid.*, p. 59. See *Mudhakkirati*, II, pp. 155-156, for an earlier speech on how every human right has a corresponding societal duty.

[106] Haim, *Arab Nationalism*, p. 44. Yet it should be noted that Haim's subsequent statement, "To use such a religious term in a purely secular context is a daring innovation, and represents a momentous departure from the traditional political thought of Islam," has a very fragile basis, for the word *faniya* and its various derivations in modern Arabic have not been restricted to the purely religious area. Al-Husri has certainly used the word where no religious connotation is possible. See, for example, the passage quoted below, p. 174.

[107] See Haim's penetrating "Islam and the Theory of Arab Nationalism."

terpretation at times tends to imply a more complex involvement with Islam and a deeper disposition to totalitarianism on al-Husri's part than may actually have existed.

It is clear, however, that in al-Husri's opinion, the proper position for the individual is solidarity with his community. Since he conceives final communal organization as residing in a unified nation, the desired solidarity is to and within that nation; it is achieved by demanding of the individual the supreme duty, the sacrifice of self to that nation. In al-Husri's frame of reference, this includes sacrifice to the very concept of Arab unity as well as to the unified Arab nation of the future. His central purpose was to establish faith in and loyalty to the present, although divided, existence of the Arab nation. Just as traditional Islamic writers urged obedience to the religious community, so does al-Husri expound on the duties of the individual to the nation.[108] The crucial difference is, of course, the secular character of the object of this obedience. For al-Husri the Arab nation is predicated on a shared language and history, devoid of all religious content. As has been seen, even Islamic history is distinguished from Arab history and religion is explicitly denied a role in serving as a basis for political organization and unity. The duties of the individual are to a natural entity, the nation, not to God or the institutions of religion. Furthermore, although the duties themselves are of a spiritual character as embodied in the concepts of sacrifice, regeneration, faith, and a feeling of Arabism, they nevertheless remain of a secular nature and are inspired by sociology, romantic nationalism, an interpretation of history, and perhaps totalitarian doctrines.

Aspects of totalitarianism certainly appear to be implicit in al-Husri's concept of Arab nationalism and unity. Acutely

[108] Cf. *ibid.*, pp. 303, 307; and her *Arab Nationalism*, p. 45.

aware of the success of Turkey, Italy, and Germany in asserting their national sovereignty during the inter-war years, he hoped that the Arabs, too, could achieve unity and respect through the adoption of selected national values. At times, such as when justifying nationalistic history, al-Husri seems to realize the totalitarian implications of his doctrines. Nevertheless, his call refrains from openly espousing political dictatorship, and does not glorify the state or endow it with mystical powers. He remains within his own careful distinction of nation, and that nation has no preconceived political organization. The loyalties he endeavors to awaken are to a politically neutral entity. As for their management, these sentiments, because inherently good, will inevitably be channeled into a favorable organization. But it is not al-Husri's function to define that organization; he simply serves as the spokesman and interpreter of the loyalties. Before the step to political organization can be made, the nation must be defined and accepted as the recipient of loyalties, the object of identity, and the bearer of Arabism. It is to the sphere of definition that al-Husri consciously limits himself.

His definitions indicate that sacrifice, communal solidarity, nationalist sentiments, and faith in unity are all contingent upon the recognition of Arabism. At times this term is used interchangeably with Arab nationalism, but in the end it is the feeling of Arabism which is the all-inclusive sentiment, the prerequisite by which the genuineness of other sentiments is classified. It is predetermined by language and history that one is an Arab. It follows then, that Arabism must be his ideology. Al-Husri endows his Arabism with a religious, messianic quality, writing at one point, "I profess the religion of Arabism with all my heart" (*adin bi din al-'urubah bi kull jawanhi*).[109] He normally avoids the use of the *fatihah*, the Islamic introductory phrase, "in the name of God, the merciful and the compassionate," but he began his inaugural speech to the Institute of Higher Arab Studies with this unique version: "In the name of God and in the name of Arabism."[110] This is not an appeal to Islamic sensibilities, but a delineation of Arabism as the ultimate symbol on which all loyalties should focus: "More than religion, more than patriotism and nationalism even, the banner under whose shade all Arabs should unite is the banner of Arabism and we should all say, 'Arabism first!' "[111] No compromise of this clear and oft-repeated call is valid, no intrusion of religious, regional, or personal considerations is permitted. To recognize Arabism is to have faith in the final realization of Arab unity.

Al-Husri was constantly aware that the material progress toward unity was slow and threatened to undermine the spiritual faith needed to achieve it. One of his most difficult tasks was to reconcile the scarcity of visible accomplishments with reasons for still maintaining a deeper faith in the future.

He finds comfort in history, pointing out that Germany stumbled many times on the path to unification. The failure to achieve Arab unity after so few attempts cannot therefore be considered final and cannot be used to justify the surrender of the idea of unity itself.[112] Al-Husri continues to believe in the motive force of ideas themselves and is un-

109 "Naqd nizam al-ta'lim fi Misr," in *al-Tarbiyah wa al-ta'lim*, p. 184.

110 *Al-Muhadarah al-iftitahiyyah*, p. 3.

111 *Al-'Urubah awwalan*, p. 190.

112 *Ibid.*, pp. 150-151; *al-Qawmiyyah al-'arabiyyah*, pp. 98-99.

remitting in his attempts to keep them alive. In a lecture delivered in 1937, he likens the Arab world to Pandora after the evils surrounded her and only hope remained in the box. He urges that this hope be preserved in the hearts of all Arabs and then adds, "It is not enough simply to preserve hope; it must be strengthened and nourished until it develops into an unshakeable faith which drives us to continuous action in the spirit of sacrifice and devotion."[113] He finds that the Arabs are discouraged too easily and fail to recognize that the achievement of worthy goals will not come without effort:

> If we examine the facts closely, we can say that the splendor of spring is but a flowing cloak which hides from view the loss (*fanā'*) of millions of seeds and the death of millions of living things. So it is with us. We cannot expect to obtain effective results from every effort we exert, but we must not regret that which is expended without apparent result. . . . We have learned that we cannot submit to the sea of pessimism and despair. Instead, we must intensify our work for regeneration, we must implant our best seeds in the soil in order to obtain all we can from the harvest, even though many seeds will be lost (*yafnā*) beneath the soil.[114]

Al-Husri maintained this public posture throughout his career. In the face of external intervention and internal divisiveness, he affirmed the nationhood of the Arabs and called for the unification of that nation. He did not pretend that the path would be an easy one, but he offered the dig-

[113] "Bayn al-madi wa al-mustaqbil," in *al-Wataniyyah,* pp. 117-118. The quotation is from p. 118.

[114] "La da'iya li al-ya's" (There Is No Cause for Hopelessness), in *Safahat min al-madi al-qarib,* pp. 118-119. This essay was written in answer to the article by Ahmad Amin concerning the riots in Damascus which had stemmed from al-Husri's educational reforms. Amin had concluded bitterly that the East could be transformed only by a miracle.

nity of sacrifice and effort to achieve the desired objective and asserted that the glories of the past bore witness to Arab capabilities for an equally glorious future. It is a future as yet unfulfilled, but the very fact that Arab unity has become a comprehensible ideal is due in large measure to the efforts of Sati' al-Husri.

CHAPTER

5

Conclusion

As this study has indicated, the attempts to reformulate old or to establish new bases on which personal loyalty and identity could focus constituted a prolonged and controversial debate in modern Ottoman and Arab history. Sati' al-Husri, as his published works and his personal career indicate, was deeply involved in this debate, first as an Ottoman and later as an advocate of Arab nationalism. Until the end of the First World War, his educational background and his career experiences were manifested in his position as a loyal Ottoman. During this period, he believed in the preservation and consolidation of the multilingual, multiracial, multireligious Ottoman Empire through the establishment of a broad-based patriotism which included all the Ottoman peoples. Al-Husri's personal allegiance was to the Ottoman Empire and he felt his Arabness only within the larger framework of Ottomanism. In this respect his stand was representative of that of other Arabs who were similarly trained and who held positions of authority within the Empire.

Yet, with the elimination of the Ottoman Empire following World War I, al-Husri made a thorough change to Arab nationalism, to the advocacy of an ideology which was alien to the Ottomanism with which he had identified for the first forty years of his life. No single answer will satisfactorily explain this change. It has been suggested that because of his many ties to Istanbul, al-Husri's decision to leave that city and join the Arab cause may have been a painful one. At the same time, however, the awakening of Arab and Turkish nationalism coupled with the defeat and partition of the Ottoman Empire eliminated Ottomanism as a viable alternative for him. He therefore chose Arabism and immediately became one of the most persistent advocates of Arab nationalism.

Throughout his career, al-Husri was able to select and utilize those doctrines which he felt were best suited to specific circumstances. His personal exposure to Balkan nationalism and his later involvement in the intellectual ferment in Istanbul permitted him to witness the failure of Islam and multinational citizenship to serve as cohesive bonds within the Ottoman Empire. By the time he articulated his Arab nationalist ideas, he had no faith whatsoever in the ability or desirability of religion to provide the basis around which society should organize. This was congruent with his personal beliefs which had been conditioned by an unusually secular background for his time and place.

In similar historical and personal terms, al-Husri also rejected regionalism as an unworkable solution for the Arabs. He frequently points to the large number of German states which existed prior to that nation's unification and argues that they were unable to mobilize their populations or to achieve the same greatness as did the unified German nation whose inhabitants were motivated by a driving nationalism. The same is true, in his view, with regard to the Arab nation. Again, his personal background serves as a complement to his sense of history in determining this belief. From his earliest years, to his work as an Ottoman *kaymakam* and educator, and even during his career with the Arabs, he never really had a country and did not develop deep regional loyalties to any specific area. Without an intense feeling of local allegiance, he could advocate a unity which cut across all regional and political considerations. As a secular intellectual somewhat on the margin of Arab society, he was able to draw on the examples of successful European national movements and present them as exclusively applicable with more detachment than his colleagues who were concerned with the maintenance of their own political power and who were often bound by local loyalties.

Al-Husri's doctrines, then, are stated in terms of his Ottoman background and his subsequent position in Arab society. As such, his work represents one of the first and most consistent attempts to explore the basis for modern secular nationhood among the Arabs. His principal contribution is the eloquent presentation of an alternative to regionalism and Islam as the basis of personal loyalty and identification. In his articulation of this alternative, he emphasizes language and history as the essential components of the nation, as the ties which bind particular groups of individuals to each other. All who speak Arabic, regardless of their race or religion, are included in this nation. Al-Husri also utilizes what he believes to be the motive power of history, explaining to the Arabs that they are a nation with a positive future justified by a brilliant past. All that is needed is for the Arabs to recognize that they do, in fact, share a common language and history and thus constitute a nation which ought to be unified. The virtues of sacrifice and communal solidarity are extolled as crucial attitudes for the inauguration of this national awakening and the sustenance of a modern nation. This emphasis on communal solidarity appears to constitute another departure from al-Husri's Ottoman outlook. Yet, instead of demonstrating a lack of appreciation for the individual in general, it represents a sincere intellectual effort on his part to accommodate the demands of the Arab situation as he saw it. It is a natural result of his own commitment to Arabism; he espouses those principles which he feels will best serve the cause of Arab unity and, for this purpose, the Arabs require a new sense of communal commitment rather than emphasis on an individualism which he regards as already too widespread. Within the context of the ideology he has chosen, the final object of personal identification and loyalty is the Arab nation, the proper sentiments are nationalism and patriotism, the required duties are solidarity and sacrifice, the ultimate objective is unity, and the grand symbol is Arabism.

But beyond the concept of national unification based on the emotive power engendered by cultural relationships, the role al-Husri envisages for nationalism remains unspecified. He does not belong to that category of nascent nationalists who "have been inclined to argue their case in part on the contribution to a peaceful world which the realization of their demands would embody."[1] Individual cosmopolitanism and political internationalism are rejected by him in favor of a self-contained nationalism. It is quite clearly the cultural Arab nation and not the political state which is the principal object of al-Husri's concern. To be sure, he calls for the coterminous existence of both, but the

[1] Emerson, *From Empire to Nation*, p. 387. Al-Husri's disavowal of this position is most clearly stated in "Bayn al-wataniyyah wa al-ummumiyyah," in *al-Wataniyyah*, pp. 73-95.

political state is secondary because it will quite naturally be formed once an awareness of linguistic, historical, and general cultural affinity has been spread among the Arabs. In this respect, al-Husri's doctrines closely resemble those of the German romantic nationalists who have served as the primary inspiration for his nationalist ideology. Although al-Husri himself was rooted in the French intellectual tradition, he unceasingly argued the relevance of Fichte and other German nationalists to the Arab situation after his adoption of the Arab cause. He believes that nationalist ideologues have played roles of crucial importance in establishing the national consciousness which led to unity in other nations. He further feels that if a similar national awareness can be spread among the Arabs, then the course of their unification will parallel that of other nations according to the action of historical forces.

Nevertheless, there are certain historical forces about which al-Husri remains silent. In his use of European models, he carefully practices the same historical selectivity that he demands of the Arabs for the revision of their own history. His examples stress the ease with which unification was achieved in various European nations once the proper ideology motivated the people and their leaders. It is necessary for him to minimize the antagonisms involved in unifications elsewhere in the world so as to make Arab unity appear natural and possible. For the same reason, he avoids mention of other developments in European history which he considers harmful to the Arabs because they contain the seeds of further divisiveness. Thus, the notion of class, since it is a potentially disruptive factor, receives almost no treatment. The same is true of economic factors. Al-Husri once told this author that he was concerned about L. M. Kenny's statement to the effect that he did not take economic matters into consideration.[2] Yet Kenny is correct in his observation. Although al-Husri occasionally mentions economic interests, it is usually in a context which blurs their diversity and subordinates them to the power of nationalistic sentiments. In addition, his rancor against imperialism is on a cultural plane and he rarely speaks of economic exploitation.

Al-Husri's treatment of politics and governmental organization reflects a similar intention. He believes that political activities should be separated from nationalist considerations and he has tried to remain above them. As for his concept of the form of government to be adopted by the unified Arab nation of the future, it has already been pointed out that al-Husri's purpose is not to propose a specific plan. Certainly, he was aware of this aspect of the future, but he felt that the path to national unity must not be further delayed by bitter political discussions. Political and economic matters will fall into place once an awareness of Arabism dominates the lives of the Arab people.

A further dimension of al-Husri's selectivity is his attitude toward the masses. Al-Husri is the spokesman of the nation, but whether that nation, even as it embodies the language and history of the people, is an expression of the people is problematical. For one who imparts a near mystical existence to the living language and history of the nation, and for one who sees the awakening of the national spirit in the souls of its inhabitants as the only means of national unification, al-Husri seeks surprisingly little inspiration from the people for his nationalist ideology. His doctrines include no catering to the masses, no appreciation of the inherent qualities of the *Volk*. He does not collect

[2] Interview with Sati' al-Husri, September 28, 1966; Kenny, "al-Husri's Views," pp. 254-255.

vernacular idioms in the manner of Herder, but instead condemns colloquial dialects as divisive. This can be explained in part by al-Husri's reliance on education as the means for a national awakening. To al-Husri, "the people" evidently means those capable of understanding his message and as such they are undifferentiated in his eyes. He speaks *of* educating the people, and most exclusively, he speaks *to* educated people. It is probable that he regards the bulk of the Arabs as too firmly committed to religious and local ties to be able to contribute to a secular, pan-Arab ideology. His hopes for the future of the Arab nation rest with the younger generation which must be trained in the values of nationalism, which must be uprooted from its immediate surroundings and taught to serve the nation. With skill and dedication, he promoted his ideas on national education. In the face of continual frustration and disappointment, he kept founding schools, training teachers, and giving lectures all of which were intended to produce an aware citizenry eager to claim its potential.

An Ottoman-trained Muslim Arab, Sati' al-Husri expounded for nearly half a century a doctrine of secular pan-Arab nationalism based largely on an interpretation of European history. He countered the diverse and opposing solutions which emerged from the First World War with a clear, uncompromising ideology. Despite the complexities involved in his adoption of Arab nationalism, he never wavered in his belief that this ideology was the only one to which the Arabs could adhere if they wished to achieve the unification from which strength and dignity would ensue. He offered the dream of Arab unity, called for faith in the possibility and desirability of achieving that dream, and attempted to inculcate the values needed to give it reality. "Arabism first," *al-'urubah awwalan*, was truly his message.

Bibliography and Index

Selected Bibliography

The Works of Sāṭi' al-Ḥuṣrī

A. IN OTTOMAN TURKISH

1. Books

Büyük Milletlerden Japonlar, Almanlar (The Great Japanese and German Nations). Istanbul: "Kader" Matbaası, 1329 [1911]. Sāṭi' contributed the section on Japan.

Eşya Dersleri (Studies of Things). 2 vols. Istanbul: Sems, Silamik Matbaalari, 1329-1330 [1911-1912].

Etnoğrafya: İlm-i Akvam (Ethnography). Istanbul: Kitaphane-i Islam ve Askeri, 1327 [1909-1910].

Fenn-i Terbiye (The Science of Pedagogy). Istanbul: Kitaphane-i Islam ve Askeri, 1325 [1907-1908].

İlm-i Nebat (Biology). Istanbul: "Kader" Matbaası, 1325 [1907-1908].

İlm-i Hayvan (Zoology). Istanbul: "Kader" Matbaası, 1327 [1909-1910].

Layihalarım (Reports). Istanbul: Matbaa-i Hayriye ve Şürekasi, 1326 [1908-1909].

Malumat-i Ziraiye (Agricultural Practices). Istanbul: Karabet Matbaası, 1321 [1903-1904].

Mebadi-i Ulum-i Tabiiyeden Hikmet ve Kimya (The Principles of the Natural Sciences, Physics, and Chemistry). Istanbul: Matbaa-i Hayriye ve Şürekasi, 1327 [1909-1910].

Ümit ve Azim (Hope and Determination). Sekiz Konferans. Istanbul: "Kader" Matbaası, 1329 [1911].

Vatan İçin (For the Fatherland). Beş Konferans. Istanbul: "Kader" Matbaası, 1331 [1912-1913].

2. *Journals Edited*

Tedrisat-i İptidaiye Mecmuasi (1909-1912).
Terbiye Mecmuasi (1914).

B. IN ARABIC

(The date of the first edition has been noted in brackets if it differs from the edition used in this study.)

1. Books

Abḥāth mukhtārah fī al-qawmiyyah al-ʿarabiyyah (Selected Studies on Arab Nationalism). Cairo: Dār al-Maʿārif, 1964. Most comprehensive collection of his essays on Arab nationalism.

Aḥādīth fī al-tarbiyah wa al-ijtimāʿ (Discussions on Education and Society). Beirut: Dār al-ʿIlm li al-Malāyīn, 1962. Includes essays on the advantages of military service.

Ārā' wa aḥādīth fī al-ʿilm wa al-akhlāq wa al-thaqāfah (Views and Discussions on Science, Morality, and Culture). Cairo: Maṭbaʿat al-Iʿtimād, 1951. Clear discussion on the role which morality should play in modern, evolving societies.

Ārā' wa aḥādīth fī al-lughah wa al-adab wa ʿalāqathā bi al-qawmiyyah (Views and Discussions on Language and Literature and Their Relationship to Nationalism). 2nd ed. Beirut: Dār al-Ṭalīʿah, 1966 [1958]. Includes a condemnation of colloquial dialects and an argument for the historical continuity of language among the Arabs.

Ārā' wa aḥādīth fī al-qawmiyyah al-ʿarabiyyah (Views and Discussions on Arab Nationalism). 4th ed. Beirut: Dār al-ʿIlm li al-Malāyīn, 1964 [1951]. Important collection of materials written after World War II. Treats a broad range of topics from Egyptian regionalism and European imperialism to Atatürk's policies.

Ārā' wa aḥādīth fī al-tarbiyah wa al-taʿlīm (Views and Discussions on Pedagogy and Education). Cairo: Maṭbaʿat al-Risālah, 1944. Presents al-Ḥuṣrī's essential principles of nationalist education.

Ārā' wa aḥādīth fī al-ta'rīkh wa al-ijtimāʿ (Views and Discussions on History and Society). 2nd ed. Beirut: Dār al-ʿIlm li al-

Malāyīn, 1960 [1951]. Contains arguments on the utilization of history for nationalistic purposes.

Ārā' wa aḥādīth fī al-waṭaniyyah wa al-qawmiyyah (Views and Discussions on Patriotism and Nationalism). 4th ed. Beirut: Dār al-'Ilm li al-Malāyīn, 1961 [1944]. An essential collection of essays written in the 1920s and 1930s.

al-Bilād al-'arabiyyah wa al-dawlah al-'uthmāniyyah (The Arab Countries and the Ottoman Empire). 3rd ed. Beirut: Dār al-'Ilm li al-Malāyīn, 1965 [1957]. Details the Islamic bond which tied the Arabs to the Ottoman Empire and discusses extensively European imperialism in the Arab countries before World War I.

Difā' 'an al-'urūbah (A Defense of Arabism). Beirut: Dār al-'Ilm li al-Malāyīn, 1956. General statements on nationalism and a vigorous attack on Anṭūn Sa'ādah and his Syrian Nationalist Party.

Dirāsāt 'an Muqaddimah Ibn Khaldūn (Studies on the Muqaddimah of Ibn Khaldun). Enlarged ed. Cairo: Maktabat al-Khānajī, 1961. Detailed analysis of the Muqaddimah with discussions of other works on the same subject.

Durūs fī uṣūl al-tadrīs (Studies on the Principles of Teaching). 2 vols. 4th ed. Beirut: Dār al-Kashshāf, 1948 [1928-1932]. Concentrates on teaching Arabic. Deals generally with the place of language in society.

Ḥawl al-qawmiyyah al-'arabiyyah (On Arab Nationalism). Beirut: Dār al-'Ilm li al-Malāyīn, 1961. Broad range of general statements on nationalism and criticisms of certain opposing views.

Ḥawl al-waḥdah al-thaqāfiyyah al-'arabiyyah (On Arab Cultural Unity). Beirut: Dār al-'Ilm li al-Malāyīn, 1959. General criticisms of regional ties.

al-Iḥṣā' (Statistics). Baghdad: Maṭba'at al-Ma'ārif, 1939.

al-Iqlimiyyah: judhūrhā wa budhūrhā (Regionalism: Its Roots and Its Seeds). 2nd ed. Beirut: Dār al-'Ilm li al-Malāyīn, 1964 [1963]. Contains a discussion of the failure of the Egyptian-Syrian union of 1958.

Mā hiya al-qawmiyyah? abḥāth wa dirāsāt 'alā ḍaw' al-aḥdāth wa al-naẓariyyāt (What Is Nationalism? Investigations and Studies Based on Events and Theories). 2nd ed. Beirut: Dār al-'Ilm li al-Malāyīn, 1963 [1959]. Important statement of nationalist doctrines and their application to the Arabs.

"Qu'est-ce que le nationalisme?" Translated by Ralph Costi. *Orient*, III, no. 12 (1959), pp. 215-226. A translation of two chapters from *Mā hiya al-qawmiyyah?*

Mudhakkirātī fī al-'Irāq, 1921-1941 (My Memoirs in Iraq, 1921-1941). 2 vols. Vol. I, *1921-1927*; vol. II, *1927-1941*. Beirut: Dār al-Ṭalī'ah, 1967-1968. Spotty. None of the flow or sense of history of *Yawm Maysalūn*. Almost exclusive concentration on events and personalities related to educational matters.

al-Muḥāḍarah al-iftitāḥiyyah (The Inaugural Lecture). Cairo: Ma'had al-Dirāsāt al-'Arabiyyah al-'Āliyah, 1954. A stirring lecture on the goals of nationalist education delivered at the opening of the Institute of Higher Arab Studies.

Muḥāḍarāt fī nushū' al-fikrah al-qawmiyyah (Lectures on the Growth of the Nationalist Idea). Cairo: Maṭba'at al-Risālah, 1951. Historical in scope. Shows clearly al-Ḥuṣrī's belief in the connection between the processes of nationalism in Europe and in the Arab world.

"L'idée de nation dans les pays arabes du début du XIXe siècle à la creation de la Ligue des États Arabes." Translated by M. Colombe and R. Costi. *Orient*, VI, no. 21 (1962), pp. 117-134; VII, no. 26 (1963), pp. 85-104; VII, no. 27 (1963), pp. 147-170. A translation of the last two lectures from *Muḥāḍarāt fī nushū' al-fikrah al-qawmiyyah.*

Naqd taqrīr lajnah Monroe (A Criticism of the Report of the Monroe Commission). Baghdad: Maṭba'at al-Nijāḥ, 1932. Seems at times petty, refuting not the report but objecting to his own exclusion as a consultant to it.

Risālah fī al-ittiḥād (A Message on Unification). Beirut: Dār al-Ḥayāt, 1954. With Akram Za'aytar and Kāmil Muruwwah. Contains two articles by al-Ḥuṣrī on Arab unity and the unnatural character of the political divisions among the Arabs.

Ṣafaḥāt min al-māḍī al-qarīb (Pages from the Recent Past). Beirut: Dār al-'Ilm li al-Malāyīn, 1948. Series of essays and lectures written during the late 1930s and early 1940s. Includes a valuable portrait of King Fayṣal as well as providing insight into al-Ḥuṣrī's attitude toward the principle of national solidarity as represented by Italy and Germany.

Taqārīr 'an ḥālat al-ma'ārif fī Sūriyyah wa iqtirāḥāt li iṣlāḥihā (Reports on the Condition of Education in Syria and Recommendations for Its Reform). Damascus: Dār al-Hilāl, 1944. Attitude toward nationalistic education clearly demonstrated.

Thaqāfatnā fī al-jāmi'ah al-duwwal al-'arabiyyah (Our Culture in the League of Arab States). Beirut: Dār al-'Ilm li al-Malāyīn, 1962. General discussion and criticism of the cultural activities of the Arab League.

al-'Urūbah awwalan. (Arabism First). 5th ed. Beirut: Dār al-'Ilm li al-Malāyīn, 1965 [1955]. Essays of the early 1950s condemning the regional policies of the Arab League, certain Egyptian attitudes, and affirming the need for Arab unity.

al-'Urūbah bayn du'ātihā wa mu'āriḍīhā (Arabism between Its Proponents and Its Antagonists). 4th ed. Beirut: Dār al-'Ilm li al-Malāyīn, 1961 [1951]. Another attack on Anṭūn Sa'ādah and his party.

Yawm Maysalūn: ṣafḥah min ta'rīkh al-'arab al-ḥadīth (The Day of Maysalūn: A Page from the Modern History of the Arabs). New ed. Beirut: Dār al-Ittiḥād, n.d. [1964?] [1947]. Personal diary of last months of Fayṣal's regime in Syria. Includes pertinent documents and speeches. A significant and engaging book.

The Day of Maysalūn: A Page from the Modern History of the Arabs. Translated by Sidney Glazer. Washington, D.C.: The Middle East Institute, 1966. Translation of an earlier edition.

2. *Articles published in the Cairo journal,* al-Risālah

The works in which certain articles have been reprinted are indicated according to the footnote abbreviations.

"Baqāyā al-turkiyyah fī al-lughah Miṣr al-rasmiyyah" (Remnants of Turkish in the Official Egyptian Language). v, no. 189 (1937).

"Bayn al-waḥdah al-islāmiyyah wa al-waḥdah al-'arabiyyah" (Between Islamic Unity and Arab Unity). VII, no. 328 (1939). In *Abḥāth mukhtārah* and *al-Waṭaniyyah.*

"Bayn al-waṭaniyyah wa al-ummumiyyah" (Between Patriotism and Internationalism). VI, nos. 242-244 (1938). In *Abḥāth mukhtārah* and *al-Waṭaniyyah.*

"Ḥawl istiqlāl al-kallimāt fī al-ma'ājim" (On the Independence of Words in Dictionaries). VIII, no. 345 (1940).
"Ḥawl kitāb mustaqbil al-thaqāfah fī Miṣr" (On the Book The Future of Culture in Egypt). VII, nos. 316-321 (1939). Summarized in *Abḥāth mukhtārah.*
"Ḥawl al-waḥdah al-'arabiyyah: ilā Dr. Ṭaha Ḥusayn" (On Arab Unity: To Dr. Ṭaha Ḥusayn). VII, no. 315 (1939). In *Abḥāth mukhtārah* and *al-Waṭaniyyah.*
"Ḥayāt al-ummah al-'arabiyyah bayn al-māḍī wa al-mustaqbil" (The Life of the Arab Nation between the Past and the Future). V, no. 233 (1937). In *Abḥāth mukhtārah, al-Waṭaniyyah,* and *Mudhakkirātī,* II.
"al-'Ilm li al-'ilm am al-'ilm li al-waṭan?" (Knowledge for the Sake of Knowledge or for the Sake of the Fatherland?). V, no. 206 (1937). In *Abḥāth mukhtārah* and *al-Waṭaniyyah.*
"al-'Ilm wa al-waṭaniyyah: ilā ustādh Tawfīq al-Ḥakīm (Knowledge and Patriotism: To Tawfīq al-Ḥakīm). V, no. 206 (1937). In *al-Waṭaniyyah.*
"al-Isti'mār wa al-ta'līm" (Imperialism and Education). IV, no. 137 (1936).
"Qiṣṣah Sāmarrā' " (The Story of Sāmarrā'). VIII, no. 344 (1940).
"Ma'ārif Miṣr fī ḥawliyyah al-ma'ārif al-ummumiyyah" (Egyptian Education in the Yearbook of International Education). VIII, no. 346 (1940).
"Miṣr wa al-'urūbah: ilā Dr. Ṭaha Ḥusayn" (Egypt and Arabism: To Dr. Ṭaha Ḥusayn). VI, no. 285 (1938). In *Abḥāth mukhtārah* and *al-Waṭaniyyah.*
"Mulāḥaẓāt intiqādiyyah 'alā qawā'id al-lughah al-'arabiyyah" (Critical Observations on the Foundations of the Arabic Language). VI, nos. 272-274 (1938).
"Naqd niẓām al-ta'līm fī Miṣr" (A Criticism of the System of Education in Egypt). V, no. 187 (1937). In *al-Tarbiyah wa al-ta'līm.*
"Shamāl Afrīqiyā wa al-'urūbah" (North Africa and Arabism). VIII, no. 339 (1940).
"al-Ta'līm al-ilzāmī fī Miṣr" (Compulsory Education in Egypt). VI, no. 261 (1938).

3. Articles in English

"On a Work of J. Pirenne." *The Middle East Journal*, XIII, no. 2 (1959), pp. 201-204.

"Syria: Post Mandatory Developments." *The Year Book of Education, 1949*. London: University of London, Institute of Education, 1949.

4. Journals and Yearbooks

Ḥawliyyāt al-thaqāfah al-'arabiyyah (The Yearbook of Arab Culture). 5 vols. Cairo, 1948-1957. A survey of educational and cultural developments in the Arab world. Issued under the auspices of the Arab League and written by al-Ḥuṣrī.

Majallah al-tarbiyah wa al-ta'līm (The Journal of Pedagogy and Education). 5 vols. Baghdad, 1928-1932.

5. Unpublished Materials

Khulāṣah tarjamah ḥāl Sāṭi' al-Ḥuṣrī (A Biographical Summary of Sāṭi' al-Ḥuṣrī). Contains principal dates, activities, and publications.

Questionnaire. A most helpful response to several questions submitted by the author in October 1967.

Other Sources

Abdel-Malek, Anouar, ed. and trans. *Anthologie de la littérature arabe contemporaine*. Vol. II. *Les Essais*. Paris: Éditions du Seuil, 1965. Valuable collection with a suggestive introduction on contemporary Arabic thought by the editor. Includes a frequently erroneous biographical sketch of al-Ḥuṣrī and a selection from his *al-'Urūbah awwalan*.

Abu-Lughod, Ibrahim. *Arab Rediscovery of Europe: A Study in Cultural Encounters*. Princeton: Princeton University Press, 1963.

———. "Retreat from the Secular Path? Islamic Dilemmas of Arab Politics." *The Review of Politics*, XXVIII, no. 4 (1966), pp. 447-476. Suggests that the division between nationalism and Islam may be resolved in a "sacred-secular synthesis."

Adams, C. C. *Islam and Modernism in Egypt.* London: Oxford University Press, 1933.

Ahmad, Feroz. *The Young Turks: The Committee of Union & Progress in Turkish Politics, 1908-1914.* Oxford: The Clarendon Press, 1969.

Ahmed, Jemal Mohammad. *The Intellectual Origins of Egyptian Nationalism.* London: Oxford University Press, 1960.

Akrawi, Matta. "The Arab World: Nationalism and Education." *The Year Book of Education, 1949.* London: University of London, Institute of Education, 1949. Treatment of the role of education in creating nationalistic sentiments accompanied by a plea for the Arabs not to neglect their specific cultural heritage in the face of pressure to adopt modern Western material techniques. By a former Iraqi Director General of Higher Education.

'Allūsh, Nājī. "al-Ḥarakah al-'arabiyyah ba'd al-ḥarb al-'ālamiyyah al-ūlā" (The Arab Movement after the First World War). *Dirāsāt 'arabiyyah,* II, no. 2 (1965), pp. 54-75. Compares al-Ḥuṣrī and other nationalist authors of the period.

Amīn, Aḥmad. "Ma'sāh" (A Tragedy) *al-Thaqāfah,* no. 415 (December 1946).

Anderson, M. S. *The Eastern Question, 1774-1923: A Study in International Relations.* London: Macmillan and Company, 1966.

Antonius, George. *The Arab Awakening.* New York: Capricorn Books, 1965. Long regarded as the standard English source on the origins, development, and immediate outcome of the Arab revolt. Remains essential but the analysis of the early genesis of Arab nationalism has been reassessed and the book should be read in conjunction with the works of Dawn, Haim, Hourani, and Zeine.

'Aṭiyyah, Na'īm. "Ma'ālim al-fikr al-tarbawī fī al-bilād al-'arabiyyah fī al-mi'at al-sanah al-akhīrah" (Characteristics of Educational Thought in the Arab Countries During the Last One Hundred Years). *al-Fikr al-'arabī fī mi'at sanah.* Edited by Fu'ād Ṣarrūf and Nabīh Amīn Fāris. Beirut: The American

University in Beirut, 1967. Treats al-Ḥuṣrī as representative of the nationalist school of thought in Arab education.

Başgöz, Ilhan, and Howard E. Wilson. *Educational Problems in Turkey, 1920-1940*. Bloomington and The Hague: Mouton, 1968.

Bayur, Yusuf Hikmet. *Türk Inkılâbı Tarihi*. Vol. II, part IV. Ankara: Türk Tarih Kurumu Basimevi, 1952. Examines a few of al-Ḥuṣrī's Ottoman Turkish articles.

Berkes, Niyazi. *The Development of Secularism in Turkey*. Montreal: McGill University Press, 1964. Excellent cultural and intellectual analysis of the Ottoman reform movements.

Berque, Jacques. *The Arabs: Their History and Future*. Translated by Jean Stewart. London: Faber and Faber, 1964.

Binder, Leonard. *The Ideological Revolution in the Middle East*. New York: John Wiley and Sons, 1964. Significant analysis of the conflict between Islam and nationalism as the basis of political community.

Birdwood, Lord. *Nuri as-Sa'īd: A Study in Arab Leadership*. London: Cassell and Company, 1959.

Burgoyne, Elizabeth. *Gertrude Bell from Her Personal Papers*. 2 vols. London: Ernest Benns Ltd., 1958-1961. Second volume contains perceptive sketches of Arab and British personalities in Iraq from the establishment of the mandate to 1926.

Burj, Muḥammad 'Abd al-Raḥmān. *Sāṭi' al-Ḥuṣrī*. Cairo: Dār al-Kātib al-'Arabī, 1969. A highly sympathetic biography, concentrating on the content of al-Ḥuṣrī's Arab nationalist thought. Written from a post-1967 viewpoint lamenting the void left by al-Ḥuṣrī's passing at a time when he and his message are needed more than ever.

Burrū, Tawfīq 'Alī. *al-'Arab wa al-turk fī al-'ahd al-dustūrī al-'uthmānī* (The Arabs and Turks During the Ottoman Constitutional Period). Cairo: Ma'had Dirāsāt al-'Arabiyyah al-'Āliyah, 1960. Detailed account with special emphasis on Arab-Turkish relations in the Ottoman parliament.

Cachia, Pierre. *Ṭāhā Ḥusayn: His Place in the Egyptian Literary Renaissance*. London: Luzac and Co., 1956.

Çankaya, Ali. *Mülkiye Tarihi ve Mülkiyelıler* (A History of the Mülkiye and Its Graduates). 2 vols. Ankara: Örnek Matbaası,

1954. Volume I is a history of the institution from 1859 to 1949. Volume II provides biographical sketches of the graduates.

Chejne, Anwar G. *The Arabic Language: Its Role in History.* Minneapolis: University of Minnesota Press, 1969.

———. "Egyptian Attitudes Toward Pan-Arabism." *The Middle East Journal,* XI, no. 3 (1957), pp. 253-268.

———. "The Use of History by Modern Arab Writers." *The Middle East Journal,* XIV, no. 4 (1960), pp. 382-396.

Colombe, Marcel. *L'Évolution de l'Égypte, 1924-1950.* Paris: Éditions G. P. Maisonneuve, 1951.

Dāghir, As'ad. *Mudhakkirātī 'alā hāmish al-qaḍiyyah al-'arabiyyah* (My Memoirs Concerning the Arab Question). Cairo: Dār al-Qāhirah, 1959. By a Lebanese Christian connected with the nationalist movement since World War I. Contains observations on the individuals in Fayṣal's Syria.

Darwazah, Muḥammad 'Izzat. *Ḥawl al-ḥarakah al-'arabiyyah al-ḥadīthah* (On the Modern Arab Movement). 6 vols. Saidon: al-Maktabah al-'Aṣriyyah, 1950-1953. Essential for identifying personalities and societies in Syria after World War I. By the secretary of the First Syrian Congress.

Davison, Roderic H. *Reform in the Ottoman Empire, 1856-1876.* Princeton: Princeton University Press, 1963.

Dawn, C. Ernest. "The Amir of Mecca: Al-Ḥusayn ibn 'Alī and the Origin of the Arab Revolt." *Proceedings of the American Philosophical Society,* CIV, no. 1 (1960), pp. 11-34. The articles of Ernest Dawn are exceptional in their sound scholarship and interpretive judgment. He is one of the few historians who has attempted to analyze selectively the backgrounds of Ottoman Arabs and the degree to which they participated in the Arab nationalist movement before the end of World War I. This contribution argues that Ḥusayn supported Ottomanism for as long as he possibly could and that political realities, not abstract ideologies, determined his choice between Ottomanism and Arabism.

———. "Arab Islam in the Modern Age." *The Middle East Journal,* XIX, no. 4 (1965), pp. 435-445.

———. "From Ottomanism to Arabism: The Origin of an Ideology." *The Review of Politics,* XXIII, no. 3 (1961), pp. 378-400. Shows the depth of Ottoman ties among both Muslim and Christian Arabs up to 1914. Maintains that Arabism developed out of attempts to overcome the differential between East and West by emphasizing early Islam.

———. "Ideological Influences in the Arab Revolt." *The World of Islam: Studies in Honor of Philip Hitti.* Edited by James Kritzeck and R. Bayly Winder. London: Macmillan and Company, 1960. Treats the traditional Islamic character of the beliefs which inspired Ḥusayn and his son, 'Abdullah, during the Arab revolt.

———. "The Rise of Arabism in Syria." *The Middle East Journal,* XVI, no. 2 (1962), pp. 145-168. Detailed treatment of the loyalties of leading pre- and post-war Syrian Arab nationalists.

———. "The Rise and Progress of Middle Eastern Nationalism." *Social Education,* XXV, no. 1 (1961), pp. 20-25.

Devereux, Robert. *The First Ottoman Constitutional Period.* Baltimore: Johns Hopkins Press, 1963.

al-Dūrī, 'Abd al-'Azīz. *al-Judhūr al-ta'rīkhiyyah li al-qawmiyyah al-'arabiyyah* (The Historical Roots of Arab Nationalism). Beirut: Dār al-'Ilm li al-Malāyīn, 1960. An account by a leading Arab scholar maintaining that Arab consciousness had its origins in the distant past.

al-Durrah, Muḥammad. *al-Ḥarb al-'irāqiyyah al-barīṭāniyyah, 1941* (The Iraqi-British War, 1941). Beirut: Dār al-Ṭalī'ah, 1969.

Emerson, Rupert. *From Empire to Nation: The Rise to Self-Assertion of Asian and African Peoples.* Boston: Beacon Press, 1966.

The Encyclopaedia of Islam. London and Leiden: E. J. Brill, 1913-1938.

The Encyclopaedia of Islam. New Ed. London and Leiden: E. J. Brill, 1954- .

Englebrecht, H. C. *Johann Gottlieb Fichte: A Study of His Political Writings with Special Reference to His Nationalism.* New York: Columbia University Press, 1933.

Ergang, Robert Reinhold. *Herder and the Foundations of German Nationalism.* New York: Columbia University Press, 1931.

Erikson, Erik H. *Young Man Luther: A Study in Psychoanalysis and History.* New York: W. W. Norton and Company, 1962.

al-Faruqi, Ismail R. *On Arabism.* Vol. I. *'Urubah and Religion.* Amsterdam: Djambatan, 1962.

al-Fayḍī, Sulaymān. *Fī ghamrat al-niḍāl* (In the Midst of the Struggle). Baghdad: Sharakat al-Tijārah wa al-Ṭibā'ah al-Maḥdūdah, 1952. By an Iraqi politician who argues that Iraqi leaders were little moved by the Arab revolt. Deals briefly with the murder of al-Ḥuṣrī's brother, Badī' Nūrī.

Fichte, Johann Gottlieb. *Addresses to the German Nation.* Translated by R. F. Jones and G. H. Turnbull. Chicago: The Open Court Publishing Company, 1922.

Foster, Henry A. *The Making of Modern Iraq: A Product of World Forces.* Norman, Okla.: University of Oklahoma Press, 1935.

Furlonge, Geoffrey. *Palestine Is My Country: The Story of Musa Alami.* New York: Frederick A. Praeger, 1969.

Gallagher, Charles F. "Language, Culture, and Ideology: The Arab World." *Expectant Peoples: Nationalism and Development.* Edited by K. H. Silvert. New York: Vintage Books, 1967.

Gibb, H. A. R. "The Islamic Congress at Jerusalem in December 1931." *Survey of International Affairs, 1934.* Edited by Arnold J. Toynbee. London: Oxford University Press, 1935.

———. *Modern Trends in Islam.* Chicago: The University of Chicago Press, 1947.

———. "Social Change in the Arab East." *The Near East: Problems and Prospects.* Edited by Philip W. Ireland. Chicago: The University of Chicago Press, 1942. Deals in part with reasons for the lack of social programs in Arab secular nationalism.

Gökalp, Ziya. *The Principles of Turkism.* Translated and annotated by Robert Devereux. Leiden: E. J. Brill, 1968.

———. *Turkish Nationalism and Western Civilization: Selected Essays of Ziya Gökalp.* Translated and edited by Niyazi Berkes. London: George Allen and Unwin, Ltd., 1959.

Grunebaum, G. E. von. *Modern Islam: The Search for Cultural Identity.* New York: Vintage Books, 1964. Includes a chapter on the search for identity through history.

al-Hadid, 'Ajjan. [Robert Montagne.] "Le Développement de l'éducation nationale en Irāq." *Revue des Études Islamiques,* IV, no. 3 (1932), pp. 231-267. Focuses on the report of the Monroe educational mission to Iraq and al-Ḥuṣrī's criticism of it.

Haim, Sylvia G., ed. *Arab Nationalism: An Anthology*. Berkeley and Los Angeles: University of California Press, 1964. Contains an excellent introduction on the development of Arab nationalism and valuable translations. Essential work.

———. "Intorno alle Origini della teoria panarabismo." *Oriente Moderno*, XXXVI, no. 7 (1956), pp. 409-421. Concentrates on attempts to reconcile the theory of pan-Arabism with Islam. Treats al-Ḥuṣrī's refutation of Shaykh al-Marāghī.

———. "Islam and the Theory of Arab Nationalism." *The Middle East in Transition*. Edited by Walter Z. Laqueur. New York: Frederick A. Praeger, 1958. A most important contribution dealing with the conflicts between nationalism and Islam. Extensive analysis of al-Ḥuṣrī.

al-Ḥakīm, Yūsuf. *Sūriyyah wa al-'ahd al-fayṣalī* (Syria and Era of Fayṣal). Beirut: al-Maṭba'ah al-Kāthūlīkiyyah, 1966. Memoirs of a participant in the period described.

al-Ḥasanī, 'Abd al-Razzāq. *Ta'rīkh al-wizārāt al-'irāqiyyah* (The History of Iraqi Ministries). 1st ed. 10 vols. Saidon: Maṭba'ah al-'Irfān, 1933-1961.

al-Hāshimī, Ṭaha. *Mudhakkirāt Ṭaha al-Hāshimī, 1919-1943* (The Memoirs of Ṭaha al-Hāshimī). Edited by Khaldūn al-Ḥuṣrī. Beirut: Dār al-Ṭalī'ah, 1967. The diary of one who played a significant role in Fayṣal's Syria and later in Iraq. Excellent introduction on the history of Iraq from 1936 to 1941 by Sāṭi' al-Ḥuṣrī's son.

Heyd, Uriel. *Foundations of Turkish Nationalism: The Life and Teachings of Ziya Gökalp*. London: Luzac and Co., Ltd., 1950.

Hirszowicz, Lukasz. *The Third Reich and the Arab East*. London. Routledge and Kegan Paul, 1966.

Hourani, Albert H. *Arabic Thought in the Liberal Age, 1798-1939*. London: Oxford University Press, 1962. An essential work.

———. "Independence and the Imperial Legacy." *Middle East Forum*, XLII, no. 3 (1966), pp. 5-27.

———. *Syria and Lebanon: A Political Essay*. London: Oxford University Press, 1946.

Husry, Khaldun S. *Three Reformers*. Beirut: Khayats, 1966. A sensitive and scholarly account of the responses of three leading Muslim Arab intellectuals to the problem of Western material superiority.

Hussein, Taha. *The Future of Culture in Egypt.* Translated by Sidney Glazer. Washington, D.C.: American Council of Learned Societies, 1954.

Ibn Khaldūn. *The Muqaddimah: An Introduction to History.* Translated by Franz Rosenthal. 3 vols. New York: Pantheon Books, 1958.

Ireland, Philip W. *Iraq: A Study in Political Development.* London: Jonathan Cape, 1937. Adequate study of the establishment, operation, and termination of the British mandate.

Karpat, Kemal H., ed. *Political and Social Thought in the Contemporary Middle East.* New York: Frederick A. Praeger, 1968. Contains a biographical sketch of al-Ḥuṣrī and a translation from *Ḥawl al-qawmiyyah al-'arabiyyah.* Also provides a background essay on the development of ideology in the Middle East.

Kazamias, Andreas M. *Education and the Quest for Modernity in Turkey.* London: George Allen and Unwin, 1966.

Keddie, Nikki. *An Islamic Response to Imperialism: Political and Religious Writings of Sayyid Jemal Ad-Din "Al-Afghani."* Berkeley: University of California Press, 1968.

Kedourie, Elie. *The Chatham House Version and Other Middle Eastern Studies.* London: Weidenfeld and Nicolson, 1970. A valuable collection of essays. Chapters VIII and IX in particular provide penetrating and frequently critical interpretations of the political behavior of those in the Syrian and Iraqi governments following World War I.

———. *England and the Middle East: The Destruction of the Ottoman Empire, 1914-1921.* London: Bowes and Bowes, 1956. An important work presenting another critical view of Fayṣal and the ex-Ottoman Arabs in the Syrian government.

Kenny, L. M. "Sāṭi' al-Ḥuṣrī's Views on Arab Nationalism." *The Middle East Journal,* XVII, no. 3 (1963), pp. 231-256. Generally thorough presentation of al-Ḥuṣrī's broader doctrines.

Kerr, Malcolm H. *Islamic Reform: The Political and Legal Theories of Muḥammad 'Abduh and Rashīd Riḍā.* Berkeley: University of California Press, 1966.

Khadduri, Majid. "Azīz 'Alī Miṣrī and the Arab Nationalist Movement." *St. Antony's Papers,* no. 17. *Middle Eastern Affairs,* no. 4. Edited by Albert Hourani. London: Oxford University Press, 1965. Re-evaluation of the career and motives of one who has been regarded as an initiator of the Arab nationalist movement.

———. "General Nūrī's Flirtations with the Axis Powers." *The Middle East Journal,* XVI, no. 3 (1962), pp. 328-336.

———. *Independent Iraq, 1932-1958: A Study in Iraqi Politics.* 2nd ed. revised. London: Oxford University Press, 1960. A standard work.

———. *Political Trends in the Arab World: The Role of Ideas and Ideals in Politics.* Baltimore: Johns Hopkins Press, 1970. A challenging treatment of the interaction between alternative political institutions and ideological concepts in the modern Arab Middle East.

Khālidī, Muṣṭafā, and 'Umar Farrūkh. *al-Tabshīr wa al-isti'mār fī al-bilād al-'arabiyyah* (Missionary Activities and Imperialism in the Arab Countries). Beirut: al-Maktabah al-'Ilmiyyah wa Maṭba'athā, 1953. Deals briefly with al-Ḥuṣrī's educational work in Syria after World War II.

al-Khaṭīb, 'Adnān. "Faqīd al-'urūbah: al-ustādh Sāṭi' al-Ḥuṣrī" (The Deceased of Arabism: Sāṭi' al-Ḥuṣrī). *Majallah majma' al-lughah al-'arabiyyah fī Dimashq,* XLIV, no. 3 (1969), pp. 447-463. A complimentary obituary, summarizing al-Ḥuṣrī's life and listing his works.

Khūrī, Sāmī. *Radd 'alā Sāṭi' al-Ḥuṣrī* (A Reply to Sāṭi' al-Ḥuṣrī). Beirut: n.d. [1956], n.p. A response to al-Ḥuṣrī's attack on the Syrian Social Nationalist Party. Provides some reasoned criticism of al-Ḥuṣrī's theory of Arab nationalism, but is mainly concerned with a presentation of the party's beliefs.

Kinross, Lord. *Atatürk: A Biography of Mustafa Kemal, Father of Modern Turkey.* New York: William Morrow and Company, 1965.

Kirk, George. *The Middle East in the War.* London: Oxford University Press, 1952.

Kohn, Hans. *A History of Nationalism in the East.* London: George Routledge and Sons, Ltd., 1929.

Kohn, Hans. "Arndt and the Character of German Nationalism." *The American Historical Review*, LIV, no. 4 (1949), pp. 787-803. This, and the entries by Kohn which follow, provide essential statements on the nature of the European cultural nationalism which was manifested in an Arab setting by al-Ḥuṣrī.

———. "The Eve of German Nationalism (1789-1812)." *Journal of the History of Ideas*, XII, no. 2 (1951), pp. 256-284.

———. *Prophets and Peoples: Studies in Nineteenth Century Nationalism*. New York: Collier Books, 1961.

———. "Romanticism and the Rise of German Nationalism." *The Review of Politics*, XII, no. 4 (1950), pp. 443-472.

Kurd 'Alī, Muḥammad. *al-Mudhakkirāt* (Memoirs). 3 vols. Damascus: Maṭba'at al-Taraqqī, 1948-1949. Treats some of the controversies and personalities of the post-World War I period in Syria.

Lewis, Bernard. *The Arabs in History*. New York: Harper and Brothers, 1961.

———. *The Emergence of Modern Turkey*. London: Oxford University Press, 1962. A brilliant work of historical synthesis and interpretation.

———. "The Impact of the French Revolution on Turkey." *Journal of World History*, I, no. 1 (1953), pp. 105-125.

———. *The Middle East and the West*. Bloomington: Indiana University Press, 1965.

Lewis, Bernard, and P. M. Holt, eds. *Historians of the Middle East*. London: Oxford University Press, 1962.

Lewis, Geoffrey. *Turkey*. 3rd ed. New York: Frederick A. Praeger, 1965.

Longrigg, Stephen Hemsley. *Four Centuries of Modern Iraq*. Oxford: The Clarendon Press, 1925.

———. *Iraq, 1900-1950: A Political, Social, and Economic History*. London: Oxford University Press, 1953. A standard work.

———. *Syria and Lebanon under French Mandate*. New York: Oxford University Press, 1958.

Mahdi, Muhsin. *Ibn Khaldūn's Philosophy of History: A Study in the Philosophic Foundations of the Science of Culture*. London: George Allen and Unwin, Ltd., 1957.

Main, Ernest. *Iraq: From Mandate to Independence.* London: George Allen and Unwin, 1935. Little understanding of indigenous forces at work in Iraq.

Man huwa fī Sūriyyah: 1949 (Who's Who in Syria: 1949). Damascus: al-Maṭba'ah al-Ahliyyah, 1949. Includes brief treatment of al-Ḥuṣrī's activities.

Mardin, Şerif. *The Genesis of Young Ottoman Thought: A Study in the Modernization of Turkish Political Ideas.* Princeton: Princeton University Press, 1962. Important analytical and factual account of the Young Ottomans.

Marr, Phebe Ann. "Yāsīn al-Hāshimī: The Rise and Fall of a Nationalist (A Study of the Nationalist Leadership in Iraq, 1920-1936)." Unpublished Ph.D. dissertation, Harvard University, 1967. A solid account. Primary focus is on Iraqi politics, but full biographical information is analyzed.

Matthews, Roderic D., and Matta Akrawi. *Education in Arab Countries of the Near East.* Washington, D.C.: American Council on Education, 1949. Examines in some detail al-Ḥuṣrī's reports on education in Syria and their influence. Treatment is confined to educational statistics and programs without detailing the ideological slant of these programs.

Mélanges de l'Institut Dominicain d'Études Orientales du Caire, I. Cairo: Dār al-Maaref, 1954, pp. 172-175. Presents a discussion of the Institute of Higher Arab Studies and a translation of its charter along with lists of the original staff and remarks on several special touches added by al-Ḥuṣrī.

Monroe, Elizabeth. *Britain's Moment in the Middle East, 1914-1956.* Baltimore: Johns Hopkins Press, 1963.

Monroe, Paul, ed. *Report of the Educational Inquiry Commission.* Baghdad: The Government Press, 1932.

Murqus, Ilyās. *Naqd al-fikr al-qawmī: Sāṭi' al-Ḥuṣrī* (Criticism of the Nationalist Idea: Sāṭī' al-Ḥuṣrī). Beirut: Dar al-Ṭalī'ah, 1966. Provides concise and generally accurate summaries of nine of al-Ḥuṣrī's works, but fails to contribute anything new on his life and background. The Marxist criticism is at times contorted and lacks objectivity.

Mushtāq, Ṭālib. *Awrāq Ayyāmī* (The Pages of My Life). Vol. I. *1900-1958.* Beirut: Dār al-Ṭalī'ah, 1968. Provides insight into al-Ḥuṣrī's educational policies in Iraq. By an Iraqi educator, ambassador, and bank director.

Nuseibeh, Hazem Zaki. *The Ideas of Arab Nationalism.* Ithaca: Cornell University Press, 1956. Important comparison of currents of thought.

Pflanze, Otto. "Nationalism in Europe, 1848-1871." *The Review of Politics,* XXVIII, no. 2 (1966), pp. 129-143. Valuable interpretation of the genesis, objectives, and utilization of cultural nationalism.

Qadrī, Aḥmad. *Mudhakkirātī 'an al-thawrah al-'arabiyyah al-kubrā* (My Memoirs on the Great Arab Revolt). Damascus: Maṭābi' ibn Zaydūn, 1956. Comments on events and participants in post-World War I Syria by Fayṣal's personal physician.

Qubain, Fahim I. *Education and Science in the Arab World.* Baltimore: Johns Hopkins Press, 1966.

———. *Inside the Arab Mind.* Arlington: Middle East Research Associates, 1960. Includes summaries of several books on Arab nationalism.

Ramsaur, Ernest E. *The Young Turks: Prelude to the Revolution of 1908.* Princeton: Princeton University Press, 1957.

Rejwan, Nissim. "Arab Nationalism." *The Middle East in Transition.* Edited by Walter Z. Laqueur. New York: Frederick A. Praeger, 1958.

Renan, Ernest. *Discours et Conférences.* Paris: Calmann-Levy, n.d. [1887].

Revue des Études Islamiques, no. 2 (1928), pp. 177-178. Gives a brief review of al-Ḥuṣrī's Iraqi educational journal, *Majallah al-tarbiyah wa al-ta'līm.*

al-Rīḥānī, Amīn. *Mulūk al-'arab* (The Kings of the Arabs). 2 vols. 2nd ed. Beirut: al-Maṭba'ah al-'Ilmiyyah, 1929. The second volume contains some observations on al-Ḥuṣrī's activities in Iraq.

———. *Qalb al-'Irāq* (The Heart of Iraq). 2nd ed. revised. Beirut: Dār al-Rīḥānī, 1957. Contains further comments on al-Ḥuṣrī's character and his educational work in Iraq.

Rosenthal, Erwin I. J. *Islam in the Modern National State.* Cambridge: Cambridge University Press, 1965.

Rustow, Dankwart A. *A World of Nations: Problems of Political*

Modernization. Washington, D. C.: The Brookings Institution, 1967.

———. "The Development of Parties in Turkey." *Political Parties and Political Development*. Edited by Joseph LaPalombara and Myron Weiner. Princeton: Princeton University Press, 1966.

———. "The Military: Turkey." *Political Modernization in Japan and Turkey*. Edited by Robert E. Ward and Dankwart A. Rustow. Princeton: Princeton University Press (paperback), 1968.

Saab, Hassan. *The Arab Federalists of the Ottoman Empire*. Amsterdam: Djambatan, 1958.

Safran, Nadav. *Egypt in Search of Political Community: An Analysis of the Intellectual and Political Evolution of Egypt, 1804-1952*. Cambridge, Mass.: Harvard University Press, 1961. A valuable interpretive account of Egypt's attempt to create a viable reorientation of its belief system in the face of material challenges to the Islamic system.

Sa'īd, Amīn. *al-Thawrah al-'arabiyyah al-kubrā* (The Great Arab Revolt). 3 vols. Cairo: Dār Iḥyā', n.d. [1934]. Constitutes an essential source for identifying the participants in the Arab revolt and in the governments set up after the war.

Sekaly, Achille. "Les deux Congrès Généraux de 1926: Le Congrès du Khalifat (Le Caire, 13-19 mai, 1926) et le Congrès du Monde Musulman (La Mecque, 7 juin-5 juillet, 1926)." *Revue du Monde Musulman*, LXIV, no. 2 (1926).

Shamir, Shimon. "The Question of a 'National Philosophy' in Contemporary Arab Thought." *Asian and African Studies*, vol. I (1965). Jerusalem: The Israel Oriental Society, 1965. Analysis of what is termed the second stage of Arab nationalist thought which is concerned with the content of the concepts introduced by earlier writers, among them al-Ḥuṣrī.

Sharabi, Hisham B. *Nationalism and Revolution in the Arab World*. Princeton: D. Van Nostrand Company, 1966.

Smith, Wilfred Cantwell. *Islam in Modern History*. New York: Mentor Books, 1959. A provocative work containing chapters of particular relevance to the issue of Islam and Arab nationalism.

Special Report by His Majesty's Government in the United Kingdom and Northern Ireland to the Council of the League of Nations on the Progress of Iraq during the Period 1920-1931. London: Issued by the Colonial Office, no. 58, 1931.

Stavrianos, L. S. *The Balkans since 1453.* New York: Holt, Rinehart and Winston, 1958.

al-Ṭabbākh, Muḥammad Rāghib. *A'lām al-nubulā' bi ta'rīkh Ḥalab al-shahbā'* (The Outstanding Nobles in the History of Aleppo). 7 vols. Aleppo: al-Maṭba'ah al-'Ilmiyyah, 1923-1926.

Thomas, Lewis V., and Richard N. Frye. *The United States and Turkey and Iran.* Cambridge, Mass.: Harvard University Press, 1951. Contains an excellent discussion by Thomas on what constituted a member of the Ottoman elite.

Tibawi, A. L. *A Modern History of Syria including Lebanon and Palestine.* London: Macmillan, 1969.

Trumpener, Ulrich. *Germany and the Ottoman Empire, 1914-1918.* Princeton: Princeton University Press, 1968.

Türk Meşhurları (Famous Turks). Istanbul: Yedigün Neşriyati, n.d. Contains a brief biographical sketch of al-Ḥuṣrī and his father-in-law, Hüseyin Hüsnü Pasha.

Turnbull, G. H. *The Educational Theory of J. G. Fichte.* Liverpool: The University Press of Liverpool, 1926.

Ülken, Hilmi Ziya. *Türkiyede Çağdaş Düşünce Tarihi* (Contemporary Intellectual History in Turkey). 2 vols. Konya: Selçuk Yayinlari, 1966. Analyzes the contributions of several Ottoman and modern Turkish intellectuals, among them al-Ḥuṣrī's.

al-'Umarī, Khayrī. *Shakhṣiyāt 'irāqiyyah* (Iraqi Personalities). Vol. I. Baghdad: Maṭba'ah Dār al-Ma'rifah, 1955. Provides detailed biographical information on such Iraqi leaders as Ja'far al-'Askarī and Yāsīn al-Hāshimī.

Winder, R. Bayly. "Syrian Deputies and Cabinet Ministers, 1919-1959." *The Middle East Journal,* XVI, no. 4 (1962), pp. 407-429; XVII, nos. 1-2 (1963), pp. 35-54.

al-Yāfī, 'Abd al-Fattāḥ. *al-'Irāq bayn inqilābayn* (Iraq between Two Revolts). Beirut: al-Makshūf, 1938. Brief portraits of selected Iraqi personalities.

[Yalman], Ahmed Emin. *The Development of Modern Turkey as Measured by Its Press.* New York: Columbia University Press, 1914.

———. *Turkey in the World War.* New Haven: Yale University Press, 1930.

Zeine, Zeine N. *The Emergence of Arab Nationalism with a Background Study of Arab-Turkish Relations in the Near East.* Revised ed. Beirut: Khayats, 1966. Valuable work on the genesis of the Arab nationalist movement.

———. *The Struggle for Arab Independence: Western Diplomacy and the Rise and Fall of Faisal's Kingdom in Syria.* Beirut: Khayats, 1960.

Ziadeh, N. A. "Recent Arabic Literature on Arabism." *The Middle East Journal,* VI, no. 4 (1952), pp. 468-473.

Zuwiyya-Yamak, Labib. *The Syrian Social Nationalist Party: An Ideological Analysis.* Cambridge, Mass.: Harvard University Press, 1966. An excellent treatment of the party and its leader, Anṭūn Sa'ādah, who held views on Arab nationalism which differed from those of al-Ḥuṣrī. Contains good introductory statement on the development of Arab nationalism.

Interviews

Khaldūn al-Ḥuṣrī. Beirut, Lebanon: April 12, 1967; April 29, 1967; September 12, 1967; October 4, 1967.

Sāṭi' al-Ḥuṣrī. Beirut, Lebanon: September 28, 1966.

Index